The Design and Evaluation of a High Performance
Smalltalk System

The Design and Evaluation of a High Performance Smalltalk System

David M. Ungar

The MIT Press
Cambridge, Massachusetts
London, England

PUBLISHER'S NOTE

This format is intended to reduce the cost of
publishing certain works in book form and to shorten
the gap between editorial preparation and final
publication. Detailed editing and composition have
been avoided by photographing the text of this book
directly from the author's prepared copy.

This dissertation was submitted in February 1986 to
the Department of Electrical Engineering and
Computer Science, Computer Science Division, the
University of California at Berkeley, in partial
fulfillment of the degree of Doctor of Philosophy.

This book was printed and bound in the United
States of America.

Library of Congress Cataloging-in-Publication Data

Ungar, David M. (David Michael)
 The design and evaluation of a high performance
Smalltalk system.

 (ACM distinguished dissertations ; 1986)
 Includes index.
 1. Smalltalk-80 (Computer system)   I. Title.
II. Series.
QA76.6.U52   1987   004.2'56   87-2747
ISBN 0-262-21010-X

To Leo, on his first birthday

Contents

Figures

Tables

Preface

The Smalltalk-80^{TM} system makes it possible to write programs quickly by providing object-oriented programming, incremental compilation, run-time type checking, user-extensible data types and control structures, and an interactive graphical interface. However, the potential savings in programming effort have been curtailed by poor performance in widely available computers or high processor cost. Smalltalk-80 systems pose tough challenges for implementors: dynamic data typing, a high-level instruction set, frequent and expensive procedure calls, and object-oriented storage management.

To solve these problems, a group of researchers at U. C. Berkeley has designed and built the SOAR (Smalltalk On A RISC) microprocessor. In order to determine the performance of Smalltalk-80 on SOAR and to evaluate the importance of each of the ideas, simulations of five representative benchmarks have been analyzed. The results suggest that:

- Six ideas substantially improve performance: compilation to a low-level instruction set, multiple windows of on-chip registers, caching the target of a call instruction in the instruction itself, byte insert and extract instructions, instructions for arithmetic and comparison operations on tagged integers, and our storage management algorithm, Generation Scavenging.

- Seven features contribute little to performance: shadow registers to simplify trap recovery, hardware assistance for garbage collection, vectored traps, addressable registers, clearing multiple registers in parallel, conditional trap instructions, and load- and store-multiple instructions.

- The language-specific hardware in SOAR doubles its performance over a RISC II with the same cycle time.

- *Generation Scavenging,* a storage reclamation algorithm developed by the author, consumes only 3% of the CPU time, in contrast to the 9% of comparable Smalltalk-80 systems.

- Despite a five-to-one handicap in basic cycle time, the NMOS SOAR microprocessor should run as fast an ECL Dorado minicomputer.

The dissertation reports two results that run counter to conventional wisdom: that a reduced instruction set computer can offer excellent performance for a system with dynamic data typing such as Smalltalk-80, and that automatic storage reclamation need not be time-consuming.

Chapter 1

Introduction

Moons and Junes and ferris wheels
the dizzy dancing way you feel.
As every fairy tale 'comes real
I've looked at SOAR that way. . .

I've looked at SOAR from both sides now,
from win and lose, and still somehow
It's SOAR's solutions I recall.
I really don't know SOAR, at all.
           "Both Sides Now",
           (with apologies to) Joni Mitchell

Computer hardware technology has improved dramatically in the past decade. Computers now cost less, run faster, and have more space for programs and data. This advance in hardware has created a demand for larger and more complex software. Unfortunately, software productivity has not kept pace with hardware technology, leading to a "software crisis."

The Smalltalk-80 system provides an environment that fosters rapid program development. The system itself was developed on a large, high-speed, $100,000 personal computer, and most commercially available microprocessors, that are much more widely available, cannot run it even half as fast. Regretfully, this lack of widely available high-performance implementations has severely curtailed the system's acceptance.

It may be possible to surmount this obstacle with a reduced instruction set computer (RISC) architecture. Such processors have demonstrated excellent cost-performance for more conventional systems. However, RISCs have an architectural style that runs counter to the conventional wisdom for exploratory programming environments, such as Smalltalk-80. Instead of an instruction set that reflects the semantics of the source language, a RISC instruction set reflects the demands of fast instruction decoding and execution.

We have investigated whether a reduced instruction set computer can provide good performance for the Smalltalk-80 system. To this end we have analyzed the architecture of and designed and analyzed the software algorithms for a reduced instruction set microcomputer *system* intended to run the Smalltalk-80 exploratory programming environment at full speed. This system matches the performance of the fastest Smalltalk-80 implementations to date (1986), yet runs at slower clock and memory speeds. The machine is called SOAR, for Smalltalk On A RISC. Our colleagues have built two VLSI implementations of SOAR: an NMOS chip (Figure 1.1) which has correctly run diagnostics, and a CMOS chip. In addition, two Multibus^{TM}-compatible boards have been designed by others to host our chip in a Sun 68010 workstation [BlD83, Bro84]. Our ultimate goal is to demonstrate SOAR in a running Smalltalk-80 system.

We have also built Berkeley Smalltalk (BS) [UnP83], a Smalltalk interpreter for the MC68010 that runs on the Sun workstation. It has served as a test bed for many of our ideas and as a source of information about the time-consuming operations required to support the Smalltalk-80 system.

SOAR is a concoction of compiler technology, run-time software, architecture, and VLSI circuit design. This dissertation focuses on SOAR's architecture and run-time support software: *what* SOAR is, *how* it was designed, and *why* it works.

- The next chapter describes the previous work in this area. It starts with a brief description of some exploratory programming environments (EPEs), with particular emphasis on the Smalltalk-80 EPE. It continues with a sur-

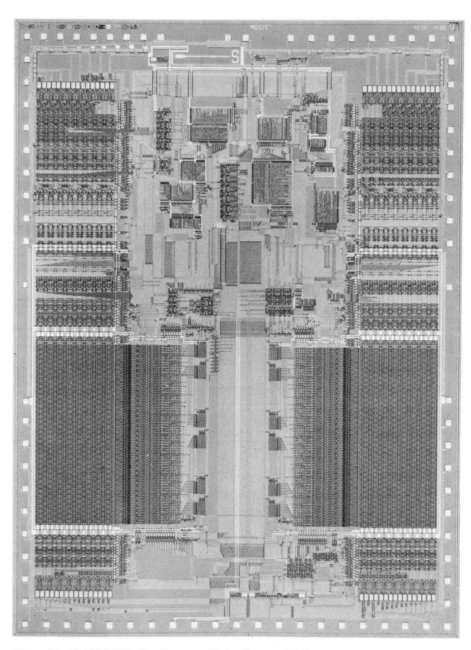

Figure 1.1: NMOS SOAR chip. Courtesy of J. Pendleton and S. Kong.

vey of architectures that supported EPEs. Until SOAR, these systems pushed the source-level semantics into the hardware, sacrificing either simplicity or performance. The last part of this chapter covers previous reduced instruction set computers, which were all designed for languages in the Algol family. SOAR is the first *reduced instruction set* architecture for an exploratory programming environment.

• Chapter 3 enumerates the problems that Smalltalk-80 presents and the solutions in SOAR's architecture. The effectiveness of each solution is represented by the time cost of its omission, based on data gathered from simulations. Table 1.1 summarizes these results.

• Chapter 4 casts a critical eye on SOAR's architecture. Simulation results show that a 400 ns SOAR will match the performance of a 70 ns ECL mini-

Table 1.1: SOAR's most significant features.	
Smalltalk-80 performance challenge:	
SOAR feature	significance
Type Checking:	
tagged integers	26%
two-tone instructions	16%
Interpretation:	
compiling to RISC instructions,	~100%
byte insert/extract instructions	33%
Procedure Calls:	
register windows	46%
in-line cache	33%
fast shuffle	11%
Object Oriented Storage Management:	
direct pointers	20%
generation scavenging	10%

computer. It will also run at about the same speed as an MC68020 microprocessor with a 60 ns clock, 270 ns memory, an on-chip instruction cache, and eight times more transistors than SOAR. To understand SOAR's speed, its architectural features are listed in order of effectiveness, from successes to failures. These results show that SOAR's language-specific features approximately double performance.

- Chapter 5 delves into object-oriented storage management — a considerable source of overhead and complexity for many Smalltalk-80 systems. For SOAR, we have devised Generation Scavenging, a software algorithm that cuts automatic storage reclamation overhead from 11% to 3%, reclaims circular structures, and provides an additional 20% performance improvement by eliminating a level of indirection. In addition to virtually eliminating the time cost of garbage collection, this algorithm allows us to remove object-oriented addressing from the architecture.

- Chapter 6 furnishes some proposals for coping with medium lifetime objects and an analytical investigation of them.

- Finally, the concluding chapter presents the lessons we have learned from SOAR and our recommendations for future designs.

- The appendices supplement the performance evaluation of SOAR's architecture: Appendix A contains a detailed analysis of each feature's impact on speed and memory size, and Appendix B gives our raw performance data.

Chapter 2

Previous Work

2.1. Introduction

Exploratory programming environments (EPE) are software systems that improve the programming process by applying computing power [She83]. In an EPE, a programmer can quickly produce either a small- to medium- size program or a prototype for a large system. The key to this productivity is viewing programming as exploration. In other words, an implementor explores alternative designs, making sweeping changes rapidly and immediately seeing their effects. Exploratory programming environments also help out the programmer by providing mechanisms to reuse code from libraries, and by integrating tools like the editor, compiler, and debugger into the environment. (We would not count BASIC systems as EPEs.)

ECL and Interlisp were two major early EPEs. ECL types were first-class objects, and the binding of a type to a variable could be deferred until the first assignment to the variable [Weg71, Weg74]. Functions could test the types of their arguments and act appropriately. These features made it possible to write programs that could be reused with objects of differing types, although in a more cumbersome fashion than in current object-oriented languages.

Interlisp, a dialect of LISP, facilitated programming by automatically correcting most typing errors and by providing tools to examine the structure of large programs [Tei69, Tei72]. When personal workstations and bitmapped graphics became available, Teitelman was inspired by an early Smalltalk system to combine Interlisp with a user-interface that exploited multiple windows and the mouse [Tei79]. Subsequent Smalltalk systems have incorporated some of the programming aids in Interlisp.

The Cedar programming environment was also designed to enhance programming productivity, but has taken a different tack from Smalltalk and Interlisp [DeT80, Tei84, Tei83, SZH85, Rov84]. Smalltalk and Interlisp minimize the length of programs and reduce the time to change and test them. This reduction in information from the programmer, coupled with the elimination of a link-editing or binding phase, places many demands on the execution of the program, which leads to the issues we address in this dissertation. In contrast, the Cedar system relies on a strongly-typed language which makes data types and module interfaces explicit. These features enhance the comprehensibility and maintainability of large systems and allow the compiler to generate more efficient code. It would seem that, of the ideas presented herein, only the storage management algorithms would be important with respect to an implementation of Ceder.

This research centers on one EPE in particular, the Smalltalk-80 system. Although other EPEs share some of its features, we will henceforth concentrate on Smalltalk. Over a decade ago, a small band of adventurers at Xerox PARC set out to explore how computational resources could help people master the programming process. The Smalltalk-80 system [GoR83, Gol81, Gol84, Kra83] is their latest achievement. We have taken a simple architecture and added a few features, resulting in a simple machine whose improved cost-performance could make the Smalltalk-80 system available to many more people.

2.1.1. Object-Oriented Programming

The Smalltalk systems introduced object-oriented programming, which provides abstractions for structuring programs and reduces the code that must be written. Object-oriented programming in Smalltalk-80 has three important aspects:

- First there are *no type declarations* in Smalltalk-80. Instead information is kept at runtime to resolve a variable's type. A variable may take on many different types.

- Second, a Smalltalk-80 procedure call uses *the type of the first argument to choose its target routine.* The first parameter of every subroutine has an associated type, and the subroutines are grouped accordingly. When a Smalltalk-80 system performs a call, it finds the routine associated with the type of the call's first argument. As mentioned above, the type is not known in advance, so this search must occur at runtime. This overloaded call also makes it easier to reuse an old routine with a new type. When the old routine uses the new type, operations defined on that type will be chosen at run-time. It is not even necessary to recompile the old routine. In other words, new types can be added gracefully to the system.

- Finally, *types can be defined as extensions of other types.* To define a new type that is similar to an old one, the programmer can give the differences, and the new type will inherit the format and functions from the old one.

The Smalltalk-80 implementation has two more features that help its programmers. For one thing, it runs on a computer dedicated to one user. Freedom from competing demands lets the system provide uniform, fast response time in order to enhance productivity. The other feature is automatic storage reclamation. Programmers of early list-manipulation systems found it cumbersome to free unused storage explicitly. Instead, they found ways to let the run-time support software reclaim unused storage automatically [McC60, Col60]. Automatic reclamation provided a very important benefit: eliminating errors caused by releasing storage too early. Despite its advantages, the high overhead associated with automatic storage reclamation prevented widespread acceptance. This barrier has been removed by faster algorithms.

2.1.2. Shortening the Edit-Compile-Test-Debug Cycle

In addition to reducing editing time, the Smalltalk-80 system reduces the time for the compile, test, and debug phases of software construction. Conventional systems require a lot of time to rebuild a large program after a change. The Smalltalk-80 system uses incremental compilation and dynamic linking to integrate changes rapidly.

- *Incremental compilation.* To reduce the work needed to incorporate a small textual change, a system must avoid recompiling the whole program. Information in symbol tables or parse trees must be maintained and reused for the portion that did not change. Most systems supply separate compilation on a module-by-module basis. Recompilation frequently takes ten seconds to a minute. The Smalltalk-80 system provides a much finer grain of incremental compilation and much shorter response times. Magpie is a similar EPE for PASCAL [DMS84]. It compiles after every keystroke. In this system, there is rarely a perceptible delay to rebuild a program.

- *Dynamic linking.* In a system that does all linking before execution starts, the programmer must wait a while longer after recompiling a module while the system relinks the module to the program's other modules. The result is that a simple change to a large program takes a long time. In systems like Smalltalk-80, modules are not statically bound together. Instead, they are connected as needed, dynamically. Dynamic linking is essential to maintain short response time for changing large programs.

• *Source-level debugging.* Although most programmers construct their programs in a high-level language, early systems forced them to debug their programs in terms of machine instructions and machine data types. Modern systems make debugging easier by presenting breakpoints, errors, and variables in terms of the HLL source code instead of the object code. For instance, they show where execution is suspended in the source code and can execute a line at a time. In such systems, the programmer can debug much faster because he has less work to do. EPEs go even further. When debugging, the programmer can try the effect of a new statement by merely typing it in. The Smalltalk-80 system will instantly compile and execute the statement in the context of the suspended program. When the error is located, it can be corrected without terminating the suspended program. It can be restarted, or single-stepped from the point of the error. With a system like Smalltalk-80, one can debug a program into existence.

The Smalltalk-80 system represents a compromise between compiled and interpreted systems. Programmers can produce more software when they can incorporate and test changes faster and when they can take advantage of a powerful debugger. Most such systems are interpreters, saving much state and interpreting it at runtime. Of course, the extra work involved imposes severe performance penalties. To run the fastest, a program must do the least work; compilers attempt to determine as much as possible about a program's behavior statically leaving a minimum of work for runtime. The Smalltalk-80 system is a happy medium. Enough information is compiled out to make good performance possible, but enough is left in to make it easier to program.

2.1.3. Graphics

The Smalltalk-80 system takes advantage of bitmap display hardware and pointing devices to support multiple windows, selecting by pointing, pop-up menus, even diagrams of program structure [ShM83]. This follows the adage that "A picture is worth a thousand words."

2.1.4. Rapid Response

High productivity demands consistent, split-second response time [Tha81]. So, most EPEs we know of use dedicated personal, high-performance minicomputers.

2.1.5. The Bad News

Why do exploratory computing environments remain largely experimental? They suffer from poor cost-performance. For example, each of the EPEs in Table 2.1 requires a powerful and costly minicomputer for *each* programmer. The research in this dissertation is an attempt to reduce the hardware cost for the Smalltalk-80 exploratory programming environment.

Table 2.1: Some exploratory programming environments.				
Environment	Language	Developed at	Host CPU	Cost
InterLisp-D	InterLisp	Xerox PARC	Dorado	$120k
Cedar	Cedar-Mesa	Xerox PARC	Dorado	$120k
Smalltalk-80	Smalltalk-80	Xerox PARC	Dorado	$120k
Lisp Machine	ZetaLisp	Symbolics	Symbolics 3600	$80k

2.2. The Smalltalk-80 Exploratory Programming Environment

In 1972 Alan Kay started a group at Xerox PARC to explore how computational resources could help people master the programming process. The Smalltalk-80 system [GoR83, Gol81, Gol84, Kra83] is the culmination of their efforts. A dedicated, powerful personal computer hosts this innovative system. Multiple on-screen windows, pop-up menus, and pointing distinguish Smalltalk-80's user interface from older systems. The Smalltalk-80 language has replaced operating on variables with sending messages to objects, and its run-time system automatically reclaims storage and finds space to allocate new objects.

Smalltalk-80's greatest strengths and its worst weaknesses result from the same design decision, dynamic binding of types to variables and subroutines to call instructions. Smalltalk-80's designers have eliminated type declarations from the language, thereby making it easier to write and modify programs.

On the other hand, computing a variable's type or a call's destination on-the-fly slows down the system, or increases the cost for a machine with adequate performance. The only computer that has demonstrated universally acceptable Smalltalk-80 performance is the Xerox Dorado [LPM81, Pie83, Deu83a]. This 70 ns ECL minicomputer costs $120,000 (in 1985) and dissipates over 2 kilowatts, requiring an air-conditioned room. Smalltalk-80 systems that run on more conventional, cheaper computers, including our own Berkeley Smalltalk, suffer lackluster performance. For example, Table 2.2 shows the performance of the official Smalltalk-80 compiler benchmark for several implementations, including a simulation of our machine. (See Section 4.1 for a description of the benchmarks.)

Table 2.2: Performance of Smalltalk-80 Compiler Benchmark.					
Machine	Dorado (Xerox)	Dolphin (Xerox)	VAX-11/780 (DEC)	68010 (Xerox)	SOAR (UCB)
Introduction	1978	1978	1978	1984	1985
Technology	ECL	TTL	TTL	NMOS	NMOS
Cycle time	67 ns	180 ns	200 ns	400 ns	400 ns
Virtual machine implementation	microcode		assembler		–
Object pointer size	16 bits		32 bits		
Relative Performance: Dorado = 100%, larger is faster					
	(100%)	11%	8%	40%	103%

2.3. Reducing the Cost of EPEs with Software Only

How can we make Exploratory Programming Environments more cost effective and more generally available? One way is with clever software on a cheap, conventional machine. L. Peter Deutsch and Alan Schiffman have built such a Smalltalk-80 system for a 10 Mhz Motorola 68010 microprocessor [DeS84], a conventional (and successful) general purpose microprocessor. The 68010's microcoded control unit implements a 32-bit, register-based instruction set that runs at memory speed. Jumps pay a penalty to refill the instruction pipeline, and calls must contend with register saving and restoring overhead. A large flat address space helps support systems like Smalltalk and Lisp that require large, single address spaces.

Although the fastest 68010 instruction is 6 times slower than a Dorado microinstruction, the Deutsch-Schiffman system runs Smalltalk-80 only three times slower.*

---

* The system has now been ported to the MC68020, in a SUN 3 workstation. This processor runs at 16.67 Mhz, with wait states [SSS85]. The fastest possible instruction runs in three clock cycles, or 180 ns. The memory system can deliver a 32-bit word in 270 ns. So, the cycle time for a simple instruction would seem to range from 180 ns to 270 ns, depending on whether the instruction is cached. On this machine, the Xerox 68000 Smalltalk system can execute the compiler benchmark 80% as fast as a Dorado.

The efficiency improvement over the Dorado arises from the following software techniques:

- *Dynamic translation.* Instead of being interpreted, Smalltalk-80 subroutines are translated into 68010 instructions when first called. The translated versions are directly executed and then cached for later use.

- *In-line caching.* Each procedure call requires a table lookup to find its target subroutine. Even though a call could invoke many possible targets, there is a simple way to predict the target of any given call. 95% of the time, a call will invoke the same routine it did the last time [DAmb83]. Thus, after performing a lookup for a call instruction, the Deutsch-Schiffman system overwrites the call to the lookup routine with a call to the target routine. The next time the call is executed, control bypasses the lookup routine and goes directly to the previous target. Of course, the other 5% of the time, the target has changed. So, each subroutine starts with a check to cause another lookup if necessary. In this manner, the targets for subroutine calls are cached in the instruction stream, eliminating costly lookups.

- *Volatile contexts.* The Smalltalk-80 language specifies that its activation records can be manipulated like any other objects in the system. Although this simplifies the debugger, it creates more work for calls and returns and thus hurts system performance. For example, when saving the program counter, a call must first convert it from a pointer into a tagged integer offset. Deutsch and Schiffman have minimized the overhead by providing multiple representations for activation records and automatic conversion between them. In this manner, they defer expensive conversions as long as possible. Since very few activation records are ever examined by the debugger, most of these conversions are never performed at all, significantly reducing subroutine call overhead.

- *Deutsch-Bobrow deferred reference-counting.* In addition to activation records, a Smalltalk-80 system allocates a new object every 80 instructions on average [Ung84]. This heavy burden can make automatic storage reclamation a system bottleneck. In this system, Deutsch-Bobrow deferred reference-counting [DeB76] reduces storage reclamation overhead to 9% of the total CPU time.

2.4. Hardware for Exploratory Programming Environments

In addition to innovative software, special-purpose hardware may further reduce the cost of an EPE. In the past, researchers have closely coupled the source language semantics to the hardware-supported operations and data types. Although memory-efficient, this approach has usually resulted in increased cost and poor performance. This section examines five computers: the RICE computer, which introduced tags, the Burroughs 5700, Scheme-79, and Symbolics 3600 machines designed for specific high level languages, and the Katana-32, another microprocessor for the Smalltalk-80 system.

2.4.1. The RICE Computer

The R-2 computer developed at Rice University was a tagged architecture with subscript address calculation and bounds-checking hardware [Feu72]:

- A wide, 62-bit word size allowed an array's length and initial index to accompany its base address.

- A rich variety of numeric types, control words, and address words were encoded in the R-2's four tag bits. (See Table 2.3.)

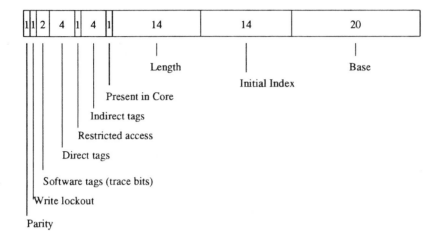

Figure 2.1: R-2 address word format. The length and index of the first element accompany the base address.

Table 2.3: R-2 Data tags.	
Tag	Meaning
0000	mixed or untagged
0001	(unassigned)
0010	(unassigned)
0011	(unassigned)
0100	real, single precision
0101	54-bit binary string or integer
0110	double precision
0111	complex
1000	undefined for normal operations
1001	partition word
1010	relative control word
1011	absolute control word
1100	relative address, unchained
1101	absolute address, unchained
1110	relative address, chained
1111	absolute address, chained

The R-2 design simplified its compilers, provided a measure of protection for the operating system, and reduced the amount of data needed by the debugger. Although it did not maximize speed, this design fostered sharing among many users in a common address space. To our knowledge, the RICE computer was the first to add tags to data.

2.4.2. The Burroughs B5700 and B6700 Computers

In the sixties and early seventies, the Burroughs Corporation introduced the first commercial computers dedicated to a high-level-language, their 5000 and 6000 series [Org73]. A tagged, stack-oriented architecture was chosen to host an Algol superset. Memory was at a premium in those days, and its segmented virtual memory system enabled the B5700 to operate with only 32,000 words of main memory. Paradoxically, adding 3 tag bits to each 45-bit memory word saved memory by reducing the number of words needed. For example, tags on data reduced the size of instructions by permitting a single add opcode to serve all types of numbers. Tags also helped with managing the stack and accessing data structures. Table 2.4 illustrates the 6700's data formats. A substantial quantity of hardware in these machines was devoted to supporting stack-based, block structured computation. The 5700 and 6700 proved that commercial computers could be designed for a high level language.

2.4.3. Scheme-79

Scheme–79, an early high-level language microprocessor, directly executed a dialect of Lisp [SHJ81].

- Each 32-bit word contained one bit to aid garbage collection, seven bits of type and opcode information, and a 24-bit pointer. (See Figure 2.2.)

- An innovative and interesting design, Scheme'79 pushed Lisp abstractions to a low level to attain the power of interpreted execution at lower cost. For

Table 2.4: Burroughs 6700 data formats.	
Class of Operand Type of Word	Tag
numbers	
single-precision	000
double-precision (2 words)	010
descriptor words	
segment	011
data	101
control words	
indirect reference word	001
stuffed indirect reference word	001
mark stack control word	011
return control word	011
top-of-stack control word	011
program control word	111

```
GC  type              datum
 |    |                 |
 |1|  7   |           24           |   car
 |1|  7   |           24           |   cdr
 |    |                 |
GC  type              datum
```

Figure 2.2: Scheme-79 data format. Two of these words make up a list node.

example, many opcodes were needed to maintain the correspondence with source-level Lisp primitives. (See Table 2.5.) As a result, microcode, microsubroutines, and nanocode were used to fit the control circuitry on-chip. Scheme'79 had good performance compared to other interpreters, but not when compared to compiled Lisp. This is shown in Table 2.6, from [Pon83a]. These data suggest that a machine that is specialized for a particular system must also exploit compilation to attain high performance.

- Instead of a linear sequence of instructions, Scheme–79 used a Lisp binary tree for program control, each node consisting of two words. The first word

Scheme-79   19

Table 2.5: Some Scheme-79 opcodes.
APPLY
CAR
CDR
CLOSURE
COND
CONS
EQ
FIRST-ARG
GLOBAL
LIST
LOCAL
NIL
PROCEDURE
SEQUENCE

Table 2.6: Performance of the Scheme benchmark.	
VAX 11/780 Franz interpreter	2 min
Scheme chip (projected)	1 min
VAX 11/780 Franz, complied (normal funcall)	8.7 sec
VAX 11/780 Franz, compiled (local funcall)	3 sec

was the instruction and the second was a pointer to the next instruction. The instruction format is the same as the data format shown above. This non-sequential format prohibits instruction prefetching and so reduces the speed of macro-instructions.

• All data, including the stack contents, were kept in memory as lists. In addition the memory reference overhead, this approach wasted time to reclaim list space for temporary values. Even with a microcoded link-reversal mark-and-sweep garbage collector [ScW67, Sta80], Sussman estimated that Scheme would spend 80% of its time in the storage allocator.

The Scheme-79 chip was fabricated in the MPC-79 Multi-University Multiproject Chip-Set at $\lambda = 2.5\ \mu$ (5 micron line width). It was 7500 μ long and

5900 μ wide. One of the fabricated chips ran small programs and reclaimed storage. Fibonacci(20) took 100 million cycles (@ 1600 ns) with a 64KW memory that was half-full. Over two-thirds of those cycles were spent collecting garbage. Scheme-81 is a successor to Scheme-79 with more aggressive silicon technology (λ = 1.5, 12,000μ w x 12,000μ h) [BGH82]. Its designers estimate Scheme-81 would run five times faster than Scheme-79. This would still run the Scheme benchmark more slowly than *compiled* Franz Lisp on a VAX 11/780.

2.4.4. The Symbolics 3600 Lisp Machine

The Symbolics 3600 is a TTL personal minicomputer for Lisp [Roa83, Moo85]. It has good performance, substantial complexity, and high cost — $80,000 for each programmer.

• Each word contains 36 bits: a two bit field for list compression (CDR-coding), a type field of two bits for numbers or six bits for pointers, and either a 32-bit data field or a 28-bit pointer field. This provides a rich selection of hardware-supported types. Table 2.7 lists some of the 34 types implemented by the 3600's hardware and firmware.

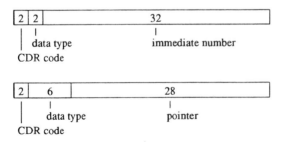

Figure 2.3: 3600 data formats. There are two formats — one for numbers and another for pointers.

Table 2.7: Some Symbolics 3600 data types.
ARRAY
BIGNUM
CLOSURE
COMPILED CODE
COMPLEX NUMBER
COROUTINE
EXTENDED FLOATING POINT NUMBER
FLAVOR-INSTANCE
FLOAT
LEXICAL CLOSURE
LIST
NIL
RATIONAL NUMBER
SYMBOL

- Each 3600 instruction is 17 bits long, with nine bits of opcode and eight for the operand/address. There are seven instruction formats. Table 2.8 gives a sampling of the opcodes.

- Some of the 3600's instructions perform complex operations. Instructions such as multiply, divide, and store-array-leader may take many cycles to complete. These instructions must also handle many different data-types. These factors combine to require almost a million bits of control store, about twice that of a VAX-11/780.

- Tags in the 3600 minimize the cost of dynamic typing. In conventional systems, a datum's type must be determined before it is used. A 3600 instruction assumes a likely type and proceeds, while simultaneously verifying that assumption against the tag. If the assumption is false, the 3600 aborts the current microcode sequence and starts executing microcode for the required operation. This saves time for operations on the most common types.

Table 2.8: Some 3600 opcodes.	
Category	Examples
Data movement	push-immed
	pop-n-save
	movem-local
Instance variable	push-instance-variable
	movem-instance-variable
	instance-ref
Function calling	call-0-stack
	call-n-return
	funcall-1-stack
Binding and function entry	take-n-args
	take-n-optional-args-rest
Function return	return-stack
	return-multiple
Quick function call and return	popj
Branch	branch
	branch-true-else-pop
Catch	catch-open-stack
	unwind-protect-open
Predicates	eq
	not
	fixp
	floatp
	symbolp
	arrayp
Arithmetic	add-stack
	subtract-stack
	multiply-stack
	quotient-stack
	remainder-stack
	rot-stack
List and symbol	car
	cdr
	rplaca
	set
	symeval
	property-cell-location
	package-cell-location
Array	array-leader
	store-array-leader
Subprimitive	halt
	%multiply-double
	%data-type
	%pointer
	%stack-group-switch
	%gc-tag-read

- An area-based automatic storage reclamation algorithm reclaims space by incrementally copying surviving objects. The Symbolics machine has paged virtual memory and its paging hardware aids storage reclamation by recording which pages of permanent objects contain references to temporary objects. Area-based copying reclamation is very efficient. (See the chapter on automatic storage reclamation.)

- The 3600's microcycle time varies between 180 and 250 ns, making it one of the fastest commercially available personal computers for an exploratory programming environment [Pon83b].

Although providing good performance, the 3600's $80,000 price tag reflects the cost of seeking hardware solutions to system problems.

2.4.5. Katana-32

Midway through the SOAR project, we learned of the Katana-32, also known as Sword-32, an independent attempt by a group of researchers at Tokyo University, to build a fast VLSI Smalltalk-80 microcomputer [SKA84, Suz84]. Unlike our RISC approach, they have continued with the traditional complex instruction set (CISC) style of computer architecture. Table 2.9 compares the Katana and SOAR designs. Katana's large microstore, variable length bytecoded instructions, and 160 registers, suggest that it is basically a Dorado on a chip. Table 2.10 shows the benchmark used for their performance predictions, with Table 2.11 showing the resulting object code for both machines.

The designers of Katana-32 are relying on aggressive VLSI technology for their performance projections. Their chip will have five times more transistors than SOAR, and have twice as many register on the datapath, yet a cycle will only take one third the time. We believe that could SOAR could also run considerably faster if implemented in that technology.

Table 2.9: Comparison of SOAR and Katana-32.		
	SOAR	Katana-32
architecture	RISC	bytecode interpreter
number of instructions	20	~46
instruction formats	3	~9
instruction length	1 word	1 - 3 bytes
data path width	32 bits	32 bits
microstore	none	4Kw x 45 bits
registers	80	160
cycle time	510 ns‡	125 ns‡
number of transistors	35,700	~200,000
*testActivationReturn micro-benchmark**		
code length	72 bytes	21 bytes
avg cycles per recursion	14†	49

Table 2.10: The testActivationReturn benchmark.	
Smalltalk-80	Pidgin C
recur: t1	recur(t1) {
t1 = 0 ifTrue:[^self].	if (t1 = 0) return
self recur: t1 - 1.	recur(t1 - 1)
^self recur: t1 - 1	recur(t1 - 1)
	}

---

    * This one micro-benchmark is not a fair comparison. However, as far as we know, it is the only Katana performance figure available.

    † 12.5 with a better compiler.

    ‡ 510 ns is the measured cycle time of working NMOS SOAR chips, including 110 ns for the unexpected jump and call delay [Pen85b, Pen85a]. (See Section 3.4.3.) 125 ns is the projected cycle time for Katana [Suz84].

Table 2.11: TestActivationReturn object code.		
SOAR Machine Code		cycles
%loadc	(r_receiver)classOffset, r6	2
%load	(r_returnAddress)0, r5	2
%trap1	ne r5, r6 /* cache miss */	1
skip	eq r_t1, 0	1-2
jump†	.+2†	1†
retnw	r_returnAddress, 1	2
sub	r_t1, 1, r6	1
%add†	r6, 0, r5 /* synthesized move */†	1†
%add	r_self, 0, r6 /* synthesized move */	1
call	recur	1
<selector>		
sub	r_t1, 1, r6	1
%add†	r6, 0, r5 /* synthesized move */†	1†
%add	r_self, 0, r6 /* synthesized move */	1
call	recur	1
%add	r6, 0, r_retVal	1
%trap2	geu r_retval, CONTEXT_TAG	1
retnw	r_returnAddress, 1	2
length		72 bytes
min time		9 cycles
max time		19 cycles
average		14 cycles
Katana-32 Machine Code [SKA84, Suz84]		cycles
pushTemp: 0		3
pushConstant: 0		2
send: =		3
jumpFalse: 10		3 - 6
returnSelf		4
pushSelf		2
pushTemp: 0		3
pushConstant: 1		2
send: -		4
send: recur:		21
pop		1
pushSelf		2
pushTemp: 0		3
pushConstant: 1		2
send: -		4
send: recur:		21
returnTop		4
length		21 bytes
min time		15 cycles
max time		83 cycles
average time		49 cycles

---

† These instructions could be eliminated by a better compiler.

2.5. Reduced Instruction Set Computer (RISC) Architecture

The machines described above are more elaborate and expensive than conventional computers. We need a machine that has high performance at low cost. One recent style of computer architecture, the reduced instruction set computer (RISC), claims to meet those demands for traditional programming systems [PaD80, PaS81, PaS82]. In this style there is a much closer coupling between architecture and implementation.

To design a RISC,

- start with a fast and simple register-based instruction set similar to microcode in other machines, then

- identify the time-consuming operations in typical programs, and finally

- take the hardware saved by simplifying instruction execution and dedicate it to speeding up the time consuming operations.

RISC designs contrast with traditional high-level language computers that rely on long microcode sequences to provide complex functions ''in hardware.'' Instead of microcode, RISC systems rely on software to provide complicated operations. Of course, software consumes memory, but we would gladly add memory to gain speed. The rest of this section touches on several important RISCs: IBM's 801, Berkeley's RISC I and II, and Stanford's MIPS. These reduced instruction set computers all point in the same direction, more performance with less hardware.

2.5.1. IBM-801

The IBM-801 computer pioneered many RISC concepts [Rad82], including a simple load/store instruction set and the coupling of architecture design with compiler technology. A sophisticated graph-coloring algorithm enabled its compiler to optimize register allocation over a fairly small register file [Cha82].

Constructed in ECL, the 801 attained excellent performance. Although this work was not published immediately, it pioneered the benefits of a reduced instruction set.

2.5.2. RISC I and II

The RISC I and II microprocessor chips were designed and built at Berkeley to yield high performance for the C/Unix environment [KSP83]. Figures 2.4 and 2.5 are photographs of the RISC I and II, respectively.

- True to their names, these reduced instruction set computers have about two dozen instructions in their instruction sets, and are distinguished by the simplicity and compactness of their control circuitry — 5% to 10% of chip area. This contrasts with 50% for more typical designs. The minimal and simple control circuitry shortens the design time as well as instruction cycle time.

- These systems were designed for existing compiler technology. In this technology, subroutine calls are slow because they save and restore registers. RISC I and II speed up subroutine calls with hardware that eliminates this source of overhead. To accomplish this, they spend the area saved by simplifying the control circuitry on a large on-chip register file, organized as overlapping windows.

In addition to providing good performance, reduced instruction set computers are easier to design. RISC I met the goal of functional correctness on first silicon, and RISC II ran at full speed on first silicon, outperforming superminicomputers using the same compiler technology. A more complex architecture would have jeopardized these goals.

Figure 2.4: Microphotograph of RISC 1.

Figure 2.5: Microphotograph of RISC II. Only 5% of the chip — the upper right corner — is dedicated to control.

2.5.3. MIPS

MIPS stands for Microprocessor without Interlocked Pipelined Stages [HJP83, HJB82]. It refines reduced instruction set architecture by eliminating pipeline interlock hardware. Instead, the MIPS project has developed effective algorithms to schedule instructions for the pipeline statically. The results are promising:

- Instruction dependencies are handled with a one-stage delayed branch. (The instruction following a branch is always executed.) The MIPS reorganizer fills 70% of the slots after delayed branch instructions. Since these branches account for 20% of all instructions, and since MIPS has one delay slot per branch instruction, there are 20 delay slots for every 100 instructions. Filling 70% of them leaves only 6 wasted slots per 100 instructions, which is only 6% slower than the (probably unrealizable) optimum.

- Data dependencies are also handled by reordering instructions. The performance of code generated this way is within 3% of the code that could be run with hardware pipeline interlocks.

- Another finding of the MIPS project is that a word-addressed machine can run most programs faster than one with byte addressing. The problem with byte addressing is that the extra circuitry required can slow down word references.

- MIPS demonstrates impressive performance: a simulated MIPS CPU with a 4MHz clock runs benchmarks about five times faster than a 8Mhz 68010.

The MIPS project blends simpler control circuitry with more sophisticated optimizing compiler technology to achieve more performance with less hardware.

2.6. Summary

The Smalltalk-80 system provides a programming environment that boosts a programmer's productivity. It does so by exploiting the object metaphor to shorten the edit-compile-test-debug cycle. However Smalltalk-80, along with other exploratory programming environments, runs slowly on conventional hardware.

We have designed a reduced instruction set computer, and added features to it to support Smalltalk. In doing so, we have followed in the footsteps of other architecture projects:

- The RICE computer pioneered tags, as a means to control data manipulations.

- The Burroughs B5700 and B6700 computers supported Algol with tagged data, descriptors, and a tailored instruction set.

- Scheme-79 was the first attempt to marry Mead-Conway VLSI design with an interpretive language.

- The Symbolics 3600 Lisp Machine is a commercially successful computer dedicated to a specific exploratory programming environment.

- IBM-801 revived interest in simple computers and highly optimizing compilers for non-floating point applications.

- RISC I and II at Berkeley taught us much about instruction sets, register windows, and data path design.

- The MIPS machine at Stanford encouraged us to forego byte addressing.

SOAR combines a simple, RISC architecture, with enough tagging to support the common cases. In the following chapters, we describe SOAR's architecture, assess the worth of each architectural feature, explain important algorithms in its system software, and propose designs for future systems.

Chapter 3

The SOAR Architecture

3.1. Introduction

This chapter describes the SOAR architecture, contrasting SOAR with its predecessor, RISC II. Most innovations in SOAR compensate for sources of overhead in Smalltalk-80 systems: run-time type checking, virtual machine interpretation, elaborate and frequent procedure calls, and maintaining many small, dynamic data structures. We conclude with an overview of the implementation, detailed in Pendleton's doctoral dissertation [Pen85b]. A summary of this chapter has been previously published [UBF84]. A more detailed architectural description appears in [SKF85].

Two *figures-of-merit* accompany each feature: *execution time* and *memory space*. We gauge a feature's significance by examining what would happen if we left it out. Thus an *omission time cost* of 50% means that a job requiring 100 cycles on full SOAR would take 100 + 50, or 150 cycles without the feature. Likewise an *omission space cost* of 33% indicates that the whole Smalltalk-80 system would grow by 33%, from 1.5 mB to 2.0 mB. With these metrics, we can find the combined impact of removing two independent features simply by adding the omission costs for each. These data are the results of simulations and assume no radical compiler changes. (The derivation of the numbers is explained in the next chapter and in Appendix A.)

3.2. Type Checking

The FORTRAN statement ''I = J + K'' denotes integer addition, and can be performed with a single *add* instruction. But, since Smalltalk-80 has no type declarations, J and K may hold values of any type, from booleans to B-trees. Thus, every time a Smalltalk-80 system evaluates "J + K", it must first check the types and then perform the appropriate operation. Measurements of conventional Smalltalk-80 systems show that over 90% of the "+" operations do the simplest possible operation, integer addition [Bla83c]. Since a type check takes at least as long as an add instruction, most Smalltalk-80 systems waste a lot of time checking types for integer arithmetic.

3.2.1. Tags Trap Bad Guesses

The purpose of data tags in SOAR is to improve performance, not to discover program errors as in the R-2 and B6700. SOAR's instruction set follows other Smalltalk-80 implementations in having only two types of tagged data: integers and pointers [GoR83]. In SOAR, the high-order bit of each word distinguishes these two types. For arithmetic and comparison operations, SOAR assumes that the operands are integers and begins the operation immediately, simultaneously checking the tags to confirm the guess. Most often (>92%, Table A.4) both operands are integers and the correct result is available after one cycle. If not, SOAR aborts the operation and traps to routines that carry out the appropriate computation for the data types. Figure 3.1 shows the SOAR tags. This feature is very important; without it, SOAR would run 26% slower and require 15% more memory (Tables A.7 and A.8). SOAR is the only Smalltalk-80 system that overlaps these operations. Every other Smalltalk-80 system incurs a time penalty for serial tag checking. It would be very difficult for an optimizing compiler eliminate these checks in the absence of type declarations.

3.2.2. Conditional Skip Instructions

Although condition codes have been widely used to decouple a test from a branch, they are awkward for a Smalltalk system. Instead of condition codes,

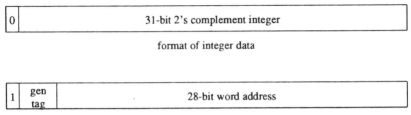

format of integer data

format of pointer data

Figure 3.1: SOAR tagged data types. SOAR supports two data types, 31-bit signed integers and 28-bit pointers. Pointers include a generation tag (as explained in Section 3.5.1). SOAR words could have contained 32 bits of data plus one bit of tag for a total of 33 bits. The scarcity of 33-bit tape drives, disk drives, and memory boards led us to shorten our words to a total of 32 bits including the tag (31 bits of data).

SOAR has compare-and-skip instructions that quickly perform integer comparisons. Remember that Smalltalk has dynamic type binding. Thus, in SOAR, "i < j" must be computed with an instruction that checks the tags of i and j as it compares them. If the condition holds, there is a one cycle penalty for skipping an instruction. If the condition fails, the instruction following the skip is executed. This is usually a jump. What if one of the operands is not an integer? A trap to the appropriate comparison software will be taken. In a condition code architecture, this software (e.g. the floating point compare routine) would have to set the condition codes to reflect the result. In SOAR, all it must do is return to the next instruction or the one after that, a simpler and faster operation.

Separating a conditional jump into a conditional skip and unconditional jump does not impose a significant performance penalty. SOAR jump instructions contain the absolute address of the target instruction. Because no address computation is required, SOAR eliminates the instruction prefetch penalty for jumps (see *Fast Shuffle* in Section 3.4). Thus, a conditional branch can be simulated in two cycles, one for the skip and one for the jump. The only way to speed up conditional branches would be to add a one cycle *compare-and-branch* instruction to SOAR. Such an instruction would require the addition of a separate adder to compute the branch target address in parallel with the comparison operation. Worse, it would only speed up SOAR by 3%, which would not justify the additional hardware. (See Section A.2.2.)

3.2.3. Two-Tone Instructions

A tagged architecture that lacks microcode must include instructions that manipulate and inspect tags. Because the Smalltalk system already relies on the compiler to ensure system integrity, we can allow the compiler to mix instructions that manipulate tags with instructions that are constrained by tags. Each SOAR instruction contains a bit that either enables or disables tag checking. Untagged mode (indicated by a % in the assembly language) turns off all tag checking and operates on raw 32-bit data. In untagged mode the tag bits are treated as data, and the complete instruction set can be used to manipulate this data. Untagged instructions also allow programs written in conventional languages such as C and Pascal to run on SOAR. Instead of providing two versions of each instruction, we could have defined a mode bit in the PSW. This would have been very expensive, increasing execution time by 16% and memory usage by 19% (Tables A.11 and A.12).

3.2.4. Tagged Immediate Operands

SOAR's immediate format has been designed to accommodate tagged data. The high-order four bits of the 12-bit field becomes the tag bits of the operand, the low order seven bits of the immediate field form the low order seven bits of the operand, and the eighth bit is sign-extended to fill in the bits in the middle (see Figure 3.2). Thus, any tagged value between -128 and 127 can be represented as shown in Table 3.1. This saves time by allowing the Smalltalk-80 software to encode some important tagged values as immediate operands. Of course,

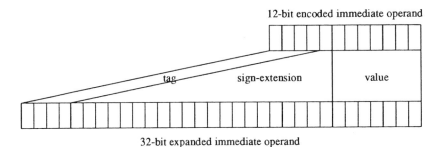

Figure 3.2: SOAR's immediate format. A 12-bit immediate format accommodates tagged data by propagating the four most-significant-bits and sign-extending the next one.

Table 3.1: Useful immediate values.					
Immediate Field		Expands to		Represents	
from	to	from	to	from	to
32-bit Integers					
F80	FFF	FFFFFF80	FFFFFFFF	-128	-1
000	07F	00000000	0000007F	0	127
31-bit Integers					
780	7FF	7FFFFF80	7FFFFFFF	-128	-1
000	07F	00000000	0000007F	0	127
Pointers to Frequently Referenced Objects *(includes nil, true, and false)*					
B00	B7F	B0000000	B000007F		
Values for Testing Tags of Pointers					
	800	80000000		assistant generation	
	900	90000000		associate generation	
	A00	A0000000		full generation	
	B00	B0000000		emeritus generation	
	F00	F0000000		activation record	

there is no such thing as a free lunch. Reserving four tag bits severely curtails the range of addresses and offsets from -2048–2047 to -128–127. However, this representation optimizes the more frequent case and improves performance by 10% (Table A.15).

3.3. Interpretation

The Smalltalk-80 system is defined by a stack-oriented virtual machine that is based on the Dorado Smalltalk-80 implementation [Deu83a]. Each instruction is comprised of one to three bytes and generally corresponds to a token of the source program. These instructions are usually called *bytecodes*. Bytecodes have the following advantages:

- The simple correspondence between source and object code simplifies the compiler and debugger.

- Smalltalk can be transported to a new machine by writing only the virtual machine emulator.

This approach has drawbacks too:

- Decoding such dense instructions takes either substantial hardware or substantial time. For example, the Dorado Instruction Fetch Unit consumes 20% of the CPU [Pie83], and in Berkeley Smalltalk, decoding a simple bytecode takes twice as long as executing it.

- Some of the high-level instructions require many microcycles to execute. These multicycle instructions must be sequenced by a dedicated control unit.

3.3.1. Reduced Instruction Set

Following the reduced instruction set approach, we abandoned the Smalltalk virtual machine instruction set, and designed the SOAR instruction set from scratch to minimize the time and hardware needed to decode and execute instructions. SOAR instructions therefore resemble microinstructions. Although such an instruction set results in larger object code, we believe that the cost of 500 KB of additional main memory is offset by an approximate doubling in speed.

Each SOAR instruction occupies a 32-bit word, and most instructions take
one cycle. The only exceptions are loads, stores, and returns, which take two cycles. The uniform length and duration of instructions simplify instruction prefetch. Figure 3.3 shows instruction formats.

SOAR departs from RISC II by omitting byte-addressing. Instead, separate
instructions insert or extract bytes from words. Unlike systems for other
languages such as C, Smalltalk-80 systems do not support scalar data types that
occupy a single byte. (The system software uses bytes to pack fields into the object header.) Processors with byte-addressing incur a time penalty due to the
alignment logic. Even if no penalty occurred, adding byte addressing would
only improve performance by 7% (Table A.17). On the other hand, the byte insert and extract instructions are critical—without them SOAR would be 33%
slower.

SOAR follows RISC II in using register-based expression evaluation instead of the stack model defined by the Smalltalk Virtual Machine. Table 3.2
shows our instruction set. The loadc and sll instructions have been cloned from
load and add, respectively. Loadc is identical to load, but is used by the compiler only to load the type (class) of an object into r6. If the object is a tagged integer, its type must be supplied by a trap handler. Dedicating an opcode to this
function saves time in the trap handler. Likewise the sll instruction allows a tag
trap to be treated differently according to whether addition or shifting was intended. Neither of these cloned instructions is very important. The loadc instruction realizes only a 0.5% performance improvement (Table A.18). We believe that the sll instruction would not improve performance much either. Since
the compiler used for these studies did not go to the trouble to generate it, we
could not measure the frequency of this instruction.

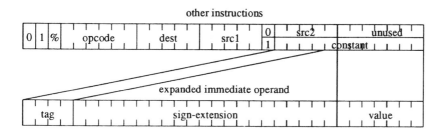

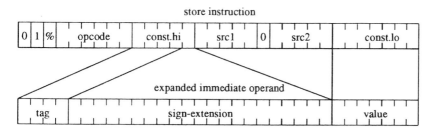

Figure 3.3: SOAR's instruction formats. All instructions are tagged as integers to simplify storage reclamation. Jumps and calls contain a bit to enable process switches, a one bit opcode, and the absolute address of the target. Other instructions contain a bit to enable tag checking (%), a six-bit opcode, the destination register (or condition specification for skips and traps), a source register, and either another source register or an immediate field. Store instructions need two source registers plus an immediate value. In order to avoid delays caused by multiplexing the source register decoders, the store instruction format moves the high-order bits of the immediate operand to the destination register field.

Table 3.2: SOAR Instruction Set.

opcode <28:23>$_8$	Instruction	Operands	Cycles	Operation
10–17	[%]ret[w][i][n]	rs, const	2	pc ← rs + const Options as part of return: [%] Disables return address tag checking (non-LIFO a.r.) [w] Change register window [i] Enable Interrupts [n] Initialize r8, ..., r13
50	[%]add	rs, s2, rd	1	rd ← rs + s2
52	[%]sub	rs, s2, rd	1	rd ← rs - s2
44	[%]xor	rs, s2, rd	1	rd ← rs xor s2
46	[%]and	rs, s2, rd	1	rd ← rs & s2
47	[%]or	rs, s2, rd	1	rd ← rs | s2
51	[%]sll†	rs, rd	1	rd ← rs + rs (Left shift)
40	[%]srl	rs, rd	1	rd ← rs shift right logical 1 bit
42	[%]sra	rs, rd	1	rd ← rs shift right arithmetic 1 bit
56	[%]insert	rs, s2, rd	1	rd ← 0; byte s2<1:0> of rd ← rs<7:0>
54	[%]extract	rs, s2, rd	1	rd<7:0> ← byte s2<1:0> of rs; rd<31:8> ← 0
34	[%]load	(rs)s2, rd	2	rd ← M[rs + s2]
35	loadc†	(rs)s2, rd	2	rd ← M[rs + s2]
36	%loadm	(rs)s2, rd	2–9	t ← rs – s2, x ← d; Repeat R[x] ← M[t]; x ← x – 1; t ← t – s2; until x < 0.
30	[%]store	rs2, (rs)const	2	M[rs + const] ← rs2
32	%storem	rs2, (rs)const	2–9	t ← rs – const, x ← s2; Repeat M[t] ← R[x]; x ← x – 1; t ← t – const; until x < 0.
20	[%]skip	cond rs, s2	2	if cond(rs, s2) pc ← pc + 2
21–27	[%]trap	cond rs, s2	1–3	if cond(rs, s2) r7 ← pc, pc ← Trap
04	nop			do nothing
05	(internal trap)			see [Pen85b]
06	(internal skip)			see [Pen85b]
60–67	(internal loadi)			see [Pen85b]
70–77	(internal storei)			see [Pen85b]
00–37	[%]call	addr	1	r7 ← pc; pc ← addr, cwp ← cwp – 1
40–77	[%]jump	addr	1	pc ← addr

† Separate opcode needed for trap handler.

Two glaring omissions from SOAR are a barrel shifter for single-cycle, multiple-bit shifts and support for integer multiplication and division. Although multiple-bit shifts may be important for driving the bitmapped display, they would speed up normal Smalltalk-80 programs by less than 0.4% (Table A.19). Likewise, instantaneous multiplication and division would shave only 3% off of our benchmark times (Table A.20).

One drawback of SOAR's reduced instruction set is the increased time for compilation. Bush has written a converter in Smalltalk that translates bytecodes to SOAR instructions [Bus85]. He reports that, running on a Dorado, the mean time to convert a subroutine is 50 ms, and that "Subjectively, the converter does not intrude on interactive system use. . ." The extra time needed to compile to SOAR instructions does not seem to pose a problem.

More significantly, SOAR's simple instruction set enlarges compiled code. Experience with Hilfinger's Slapdash SOAR compiler suggests that on the average, one bytecode results in one 32-bit SOAR instruction. Thus, ignoring data objects, object headers, and literal data within subroutines, there is a fourfold code expansion. However, bytecodes constitute only about one eighth of a 32-bit Smalltalk-80 image, and the net increase is only 0.5 MB over the original 1 MB. This is not an exorbitant price to pay given current memory technology.

Other compiled Smalltalk-80 systems also pay this price. The Xerox 68010 system devotes 0.25 MB to a cache of compiled code [DeS84]. Deutsch reports that one bytcode results in six bytes of MC68010 instructions, which is worse than the factor of 4 for SOAR [Deu85]. This means that if it were to compile all of the code, as the SOAR system does, the Xerox 68010 system would need 0.7 MB (Table 3.3).

Finally, our decision to abandon bytecodes will force us to rewrite the Smalltalk-80 debugger. Lee has designed a debugger for SOAR and has built a prototype in Berkeley Smalltalk [Lee84]. He exploited the hardware organization of SOAR in the design of the debugger to add a conditional breakpoint facility and increase execution speed during debugging.

3.3.2. SOAR Interrupts and Traps

Interrupts and traps play a larger role in SOAR than in RISC II. Unlike C, Smalltalk grew in an environment with extensive, system-specific microcode. Since SOAR has no microcode, unusual situations must be met with a trap to a software handler. For example, as described above, other Smalltalk implementations check the types of arithmetic operands sequentially, before performing the operation. SOAR checks in parallel, trapping if the operands are not simple integers. These account for about half of the traps (Table A.25).

How valuable are conditional trap instructions? They save time and space by replacing a two-cycle two-instruction sequence with one single-cycle instruction. For instance, the prologue in each subroutine uses a conditional trap instruction that verifies the type of its first argument. This saves a cycle over a

Table 3.3: Space Penalty of Compilation.			
System	execution model	code expansion	image size*
Berkeley Smalltalk	bytecode interpreter	1:1	1.0 MB
Xerox 68010	cache of compiled code	6:1	1.3 MB
SOAR	compiles everything	4:1	1.5 MB
hypothetical 68010	compiles everything	6:1	1.7 MB

* excluding transient objects.

skip and branch in the common case. Trap instructions also support type checking in low-level primitive routines, and tag checking for automatic storage reclamation. However, if the trap instruction traps, it takes more time to handle the
trap than the jump from a skip-and-jump sequence. In fact, trap instructions account for 10% of the traps (Table A.25). Despite all these uses, the savings from
trap instructions does not add up to much; SOAR would run only 4% slower and
require only 2% more memory without them (Tables A.23 and A.24). The fact
that trap instructions save little time results more from the low frequency of trap
instructions than from the penalty associated with taking the traps.

The remaining source of traps also arises in RISC II. A call or return that
exceeds the on-chip register window capacity must trap to a routine to save or
restore a set of registers. This accounts for the remaining 40% of the traps
(Table A.25).

To reduce the cost of trapping, SOAR exploits *shadow registers* that catch
the operands of the trapping instruction. These are inexpensive in single-chip
processors; they are just two more registers on the data busses near the ALU.
This feature is insignificant; without it, SOAR would run only 0.04% slower and
require no more memory (Table A.26). Other features that simplify trap handling include simple instructions and uniform instruction size.

SOAR does not support nested interrupts or traps because they complicate
the architecture. The interrupt-enable bit in the PSW (Figure 3.4) is reset upon
an interrupt or trap. Each trap handler first captures any necessary machine
state, then re-enables interrupts. Most handlers need their own register window
to hold this state. The normal method to obtain a new register window would be
to execute a call instruction but, since a call can cause a trap (see above), the trap
handler must simulate the call (and trap). After getting a new window and

saving the machine state, the handler can re-enable interrupts (and optionally surrender its register window) with a form of the return instruction.

When an interrupt or trap occurs, the instruction that is executing is aborted before it can change any registers. The address of the aborted instruction is saved in r7. I/O interrupts are disabled by clearing the interrupt enable bit in the PSW. This freezes the shadow registers, which normally track the ALU inputs. A vector is constructed from the trap base register, the opcode of the aborted instruction, and the reason for the trap. Finally, control is transferred to the vectored location. Table 3.4 lists the various categories of traps, with interrupt priority listed from highest to lowest.

Many instructions can trap for several reasons at once. To simplify the interface to the trap handler code, the reasons are prioritized. After handling a trap, the offending instruction is typically reexecuted to spring any remaining traps. Table 3.5 shows which reasons apply to which instructions. If instead of vectoring, SOAR put the reason for the trap in a special register the system would be only 3% slower (Table A.28).

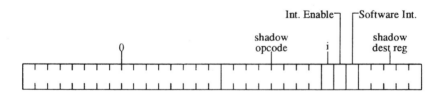

Figure 3.4: SOAR Program Status Word. The SOAR program status word contains a destination register shadow field, an opcode shadow field, and enable bits for external and software interrupts.

Table 3.4: SOAR traps and interrupts.			
Name	*Vector*	*Pri Class*	*Explanation*
Illegal Opcode (ILL)	0	A	I<31>=1 or I<28:23> = unused
Tag Trap (TT)	1	B	See [SKF85].
Software Interrupt (SWI)	2	B	I<30:29> = 01 and psw<5> = 1
Window Overflow (WO)	3	C	I = call and cwp<6:4> - 1 = swp<6:4>
Window Underflow (WU)	4	C	I = ret and cwp<6:4> + 1 = swp<6:4>
Data Page Fault (DPF)	5	C	page fault pin asserted during data memory access
Trap Instruction (TI)	6	C	I = trap instruction & condition is true
Generation Scavenging (GS)	7	D	See [SKF85].
Instruction Page Fault (IPF)	8	E	page fault pin asserted during I-fetch of next instruction
Input/Output (IO)	9	F	I/O interrupt pin asserted during I-fetch of next instruction

Table 3.5: Trap reasons by instruction category.					
	A	B	C	D	E
Call	ILL	SWI	WO		IPF
Jump	ILL	SWI			IPF
Return	ILL		WU	GS	IPF
ALU	ILL	TT			IPF
Skip	ILL	TT			IPF
Trap	ILL	TT	TI		IPF
Shift	ILL	TT			IPF
Load	ILL	TT	DPF		IPF
Store	ILL	TT	DPF	GS	IPF
Byte	ILL				IPF

When SOAR does trap, it expends two extra cycles to flush the pipeline. A one-cycle trap, while feasible, would have significantly degraded the cycle time [Pen85b]. Since the extra trap cycle increased the number of cycles by less than one percent, the net result was a faster system.

3.4. Fast Calls

The Smalltalk-80 system stresses program modularity, but omits macros because they would make it harder to incorporate changes quickly. If the user
changed a macro, the system would have to recompile all of the modules that in-
stantiated it. This would make it more difficult to maintain the split-second
response time that is crucial to highly productive programming. Instead,
Smalltalk-80 programs are broken up into many small subroutines. Consequently, Smalltalk-80 systems execute a higher percentage of call instructions than
most other systems. In addition to being frequent, calls are also expensive because:

- To aid program debugging, Smalltalk-80 initializes all local variables on each
  call.

- A consequence of Smalltalk-80's power is that the destination of a call is
  recomputed from the type of the first argument, with a table lookup each time
  the call is executed.

The result is that many Smalltalk implementations (including Berkeley Smalltalk
and Dorado Smalltalk) spend about half of their time on calls and returns
[Deu81]. SOAR reduces the Smalltalk call/return overhead in several ways.

3.4.1. Multiple Overlapping On-Chip Register Windows

SOAR, like RISC I, optimizes subroutine calls and returns by providing a
large, on-chip register file. The registers are divided up into overlapping windows. Instead of saving or restoring registers, calls or returns merely switch
windows (Figure 3.5). Compared to C language subroutines, the shorter
Smalltalk subroutines pass fewer operands and use fewer local variables, and so
need fewer registers. For this reason, each SOAR register window has eight registers instead of 12 for RISC I. Figures 3.6 and 3.7 show the register organiza-

tion of SOAR. In addition to 56 more registers, the inclusion of register windows results in the addition of a register to select the current window (the Current Window Pointer, or cwp), a register to detect overflows by recording the last saved window (Saved Window Pointer, or swp), more elaborate register decoders, and trapping logic [Pen85b]. Despite the cost of all the added hardware, Smalltalk-80's predilection for procedure calls makes this feature very important. The cost of saving and restoring a conventional register file would slow the machine down by 46%, even with load- and store-multiple instructions (Table A.29).

When the number of activations on the stack exceeds the on-chip register capacity, SOAR traps to a software routine that saves the contents of a set of registers in memory. Unlike RISC II, SOAR has load- and store-multiple instructions to speed register saving and restoring. These instructions can transfer eight registers in nine cycles (one instruction fetch and eight data accesses). Without them, the system would need eight individual instructions that would consume sixteen cycles (eight instruction fetches plus eight data accesses). Load- and store-multiple are also helpful for garbage collection, copying data, and operations on bit-mapped images. These instructions have the ability to operate on non-contiguous data; the increment between memory references is given by the SOURCE2 field. In retrospect, these multi-cycle instructions added some complexity to the design, and the benefits — 3% of execution time and 2% of memory — may not be worth the costs (Tables A.33 and A.34).

3.4.2. Caching Call Targets In Line

Another way SOAR reduces subroutine overhead is by decreasing the time taken to find the target of a call. Once computed, the target's address is cached in the instruction stream for subsequent use, as suggested by Schiffman and Deutsch [DeS84]. Figures 3.8 and 3.9 illustrate this idea. This in-line caching

Physical Registers   *Logical Registers*

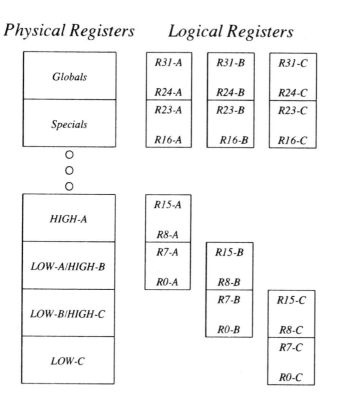

Figure 3.6: SOAR's register windows. Like RISC I, SOAR has many physical sets of registers that map to the logical registers seen by each subroutine.

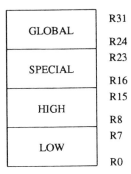

Figure 3.7: Logical view of register file. The HIGHs hold incoming parameters and local variables. The LOWs are for outgoing arguments. The SPECIALs include the PSW and a register that always contains zero. The GLOBALs are for system software such as trap handlers.

exacts a price for its time savings; SOAR must support non-reentrant code. Since all Smalltalk processes share the same address space, process switches must be avoided in sections of code that modify or use the cached data. One approach would be to implement semaphores in software. This would be too expensive because each Smalltalk call executes a short non-reentrant section of code. The approach we followed was to add a bit to each instruction to disable process switches.

In Smalltalk, calls and jumps are so frequent that the virtual machine can defer a process switch until executing the next call or jump instruction. The SOAR call and jump instructions include a bit to specify when it is safe to switch processes [Deu82b]. This bit enables a *software interrupt.* When the operating system desires a process switch, it sets a bit in the Program Status Word requesting the software interrupt and resumes execution of the same process. The next time a safe jump or call is executed, the software interrupt transfers control to the operating system which can then safely suspend the process.

BEFORE

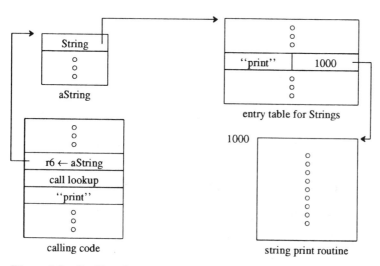

Figure 3.8: Caching the target address in the instruction stream. In this example, the print routine is called with an argument that is a string. (The argument is passed in r6.) The first time the call instruction is executed, the call contains the address of a lookup routine and the word after the call contains a pointer to the name "print." The lookup routine follows the pointers to the entry table for strings, and finds the entry for "print." It then overwrites the call instruction with a call to that routine and replaces the word after the call with the type of the argument (string).

AFTER

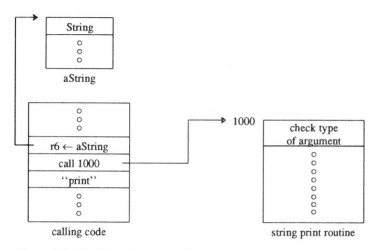

Figure 3.9: Caching the target address in the instruction stream. The next time the call is executed, control goes directly to the string print routine. A prologue checks that the current argument's type matches the contents of the word following the call instruction. This word contains the type that the argument had the previous time the call was executed. If the types match, control falls through to the string print routine, otherwise another table lookup is needed.

Although complicated, in-line caching pays handsome rewards. The conventional way to cache call targets is a hash table. But the overhead for probing into a hash table would slow SOAR by 33% (Table A.37). The hardware penalty for in-line caching is the software trap mechanism. If we were forced to omit this, we could use an *indirect* in-line cache. The informations could be cached in a per-process data area instead of the call instruction. This would slow SOAR down by 7% (Table A.37). Even with in-line caching, SOAR still spends 11% of its time in cache probes and another 12% handling misses. Further research into computing the target of the call could yield substantial savings.

3.4.3. Fast Shuffle: One Cycle Calls and Jumps

Finally, the call instruction itself has been designed for rapid execution. In most architectures, a call requires an address computation (typically the addition of an offset to a base register). This forces the call to take an extra cycle because its target cannot be prefetched. In SOAR, the call instruction contains the absolute address of its destination. Furthermore, a call (or jump) can be recognized easily by examining only one bit. This makes it possible to detect these instructions in time to send the incoming data back to the memory as an address. This way, a call or jump on SOAR executes at full speed requiring only one cycle. This "Fast Shuffle" mechanism combines on-chip logic to detect calls and jumps with and an off-chip latch to store the incoming instruction and send it back to memory. Figure 3.10 illustrates the Fast Shuffle logic. Though not spectacular, its performance impact is significant. SOAR would use 11% more cycles without the Fast Shuffle.

Pendleton has uncovered a serious flaw in our realization of the Fast Shuffle [Pen85a]. When a jump or call instruction follows a skip, the skip condition must be evaluated before the chip can signal a Fast Shuffle to the memory system. If the condition holds, the memory system must use the PC as the address of the next instruction; if the conditon fails the memory system must use the target field from the jump or call instruction. In designing the instruction set, we encoded the condition field (of skip and trap) so tightly that a PLA was required to decode the condition and the output of the ALU. This PLA adds 110 ns to the time needed to compute the Fast Shuffle control signal during a skip instruction. Although the NMOS SOAR chips can execute an instruction in 400 ns, the memory system can not start the next instruction fetch for another 100 ns, reducing the effective cycle time to about 510 ns. This overhead could be eliminated by foregoing the Fast Shuffle and using delayed branches and calls. Alternatively, the instruction set could be redesigned with a condition field that could be decoded more quickly. This problem would have been found much earlier if we had simulated the whole system instead of the processor.

3.4.4. The Return Instruction: Parallel Register Initialization

The other half of the team is the return instruction. In SOAR, the return instruction performs one compulsory and three optional functions, specified by the low-order three opcode bits. The compulsory function is a transfer of control, which means that the bare-bones return instruction can be used as an indirect jump. If tag checking is enabled, the tag of the return address is checked. This provides a means to intercept returns when the activation record must be saved. The first optional function enables interrupts and yields a "return from inter-

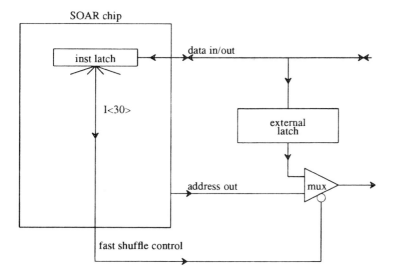

Figure 3.10: Fast Shuffle logic. When a call or jump is fetched from memory, the next instruction is prefetched based on the external address latch instead of the PC.

rupt'' instruction. The second optional function increments the cwp (changing register windows) for returning from a normal call.

The Smalltalk-80 language requires local variables to be initialized to nil, so the last optional function for SOAR's return instruction prepares registers 8 through 13 for a future call by writing nil into them. Instead of commencing each subroutine with an instruction sequence to write nil into each register that will contain a local variable, SOAR exploits VLSI circuitry to initialize the registers in parallel. Although it would be more straightforward for the call instruction to perform this initialization, this would slow down the call. Instead, we have placed this functionality in the return instruction. Since the return instruction must wait an extra cycle to fetch its target instruction, the ''nilling'' does not slow the instruction down. This feature eliminates the extra time required to initialize the registers after every call. Ironically, Smalltalk-80 subroutines use so few temporary variables — less than one on the average — that this feature has little favorable impact. The system would only run 4.3% slower and use 1% more memory without it.

3.5. Object-Oriented Storage Management

Smalltalk-80 data structures are called objects. SOAR objects average 14 words in length and live for about 500 instructions. Smalltalk-80 objects are smaller and more volatile than data structures in most other exploratory programming environments. Smalltalk-80 systems face three challenges in managing storage for objects:

- *Automatic storage reclamation* — On average, 12 words of data are freed and must be reclaimed per 100 Smalltalk-80 virtual machine bytecodes executed.

- *Virtual memory* — All objects must be in the same address space.

• *Object-relative addressing* — Although offsets into objects are known at compile-time, base addresses are not. Code must be compiled to address fields relative to dynamically determined base addresses.

3.5.1. Automatic Storage Reclamation

SOAR supports Generation Scavenging to reclaim storage efficiently without requiring costly indirection or reference counting (see Section 5.8). This algorithm is based on the observation that most objects either die young or live forever. Thus, objects are placed into two generations and only new objects are reclaimed. A better method of storage reclamation has a strong impact on performance; most other algorithms would squander 10% to 15% of SOAR's time on automatic storage reclamation instead of Generation Scavenging's 3%. (see Chapter 5). Hence, without Generation Scavenging SOAR would take 4% to 15% more cycles to run the benchmarks.

Traditional software and microcode implementations of object-oriented systems rely on an object address table (Figure 3.11). Each field of an object contains an index into this table, and the table entry contains the address of each object. The level of indirection supplied by the table provides support for compaction. As explained in Chapter 5, Generation Scavenging provides compaction for free, permitting SOAR to function without an object table (Figure 3.12). Without this algorithm, the extra work to follow the indirect pointers through the object table would slow SOAR down by 20% (Section 5.9.4).

Generation Scavenging requires that a list be updated whenever a pointer to a new object is stored in an old object. When designing SOAR, we thought that stores would be frequent enough to warrant hardware support for this check. Thus SOAR tags each pointer with the generation of the object that it points to. While computing the memory address, the store instruction compares the generation tag of the data being stored with the generation tag of the memory ad-

BEFORE

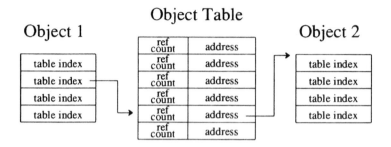

Figure 3.11: Indirect addressing. In traditional Smalltalk-80 systems, each pointer is really a table index. The table entry contains the target's reference count and memory address. This indirection required previous Smalltalk-80 systems to dedicate base registers to frequently accessed objects. The overhead to update these registers slowed each procedure call and return.

AFTER

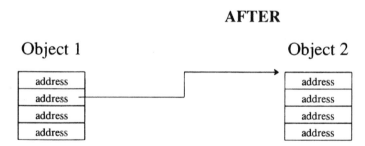

Figure 3.12: Direct addressing. A SOAR pointer contain the virtual address of the target object. This is the fastest way to follow pointers.

dress (Figure 3.13). For 96% of the stores, list update is unnecessary and the store completes without trapping (Table A.52). Once again we rely on tags to confirm the normal case and trap in the unusual case. Surprisingly, tagged stores are so infrequent that hardware support saves only 1% of the time and 3% of memory over an explicit check (Tables A.49 and A.51). This feature does not seem to be worth the effort.

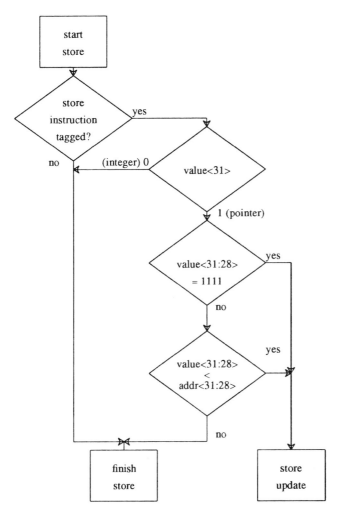

Figure 3.13: Generation tag checking in parallel with a store operation. The first check (= 1111) is for contexts and is explained in Section 3.5.2.

3.5.2. Activation Records as Objects

Smalltalk-80 activation records pose a special problem. Since each call needs a new activation record, they must be easy to create. Because local variables reside in them, at least the current activation record must be easy to access. For these reasons, high-performance systems for other languages allocate activation records on a stack, and keep the active activation record in registers. The problem for Smalltalk-80 systems arises because the language specifies that the format and lifetime of an activation record shall be the same as any other object. In other words, a Smalltalk-80 activation record must be stored in memory with a standard object header. Worse, an activation record cannot be deallocated until the last reference to it is destroyed — even after control returns from it.

SOAR caches activation records in an on-chip register file for speed, backed with an overflow stack in memory. Pointers to activation records are rare, so SOAR's hardware merely detects these and causes a trap at the appropriate time. The first trap occurs when a reference to an activation record is created. Pointers to activation records have all the tag bits set. When such a word is stored into memory, the tag check causes a trap. At the time of the trap, the high order bit of the activation record's return address is set. Setting this bit indicates that the activation record may outlive its parent. Since these records are normally allocated and freed last-in-first-out (LIFO), we label such anomalously long-lived activation records as *non-LIFO*. The return instruction then traps if the return address has the high order bit set — this lets software save this activation record in the heap.

What if a program references an activation record while it is still on the stack? First, SOAR leaves small gaps between activation records when they are stored in main memory. These gaps are initialized with object headers to permit the stored activation records to behave as objects. Second, SOAR's hardware provides pointer-to-register addressing. Each load and store checks if the target address resides in the on-chip register file. If so, the chip substitutes a register access for a memory access. This mechanism makes it possible to access on-chip activation records as if they were in memory.

Since designing SOAR, we have come up with a software solution to the pointer-to-register problem. This scheme eliminates the comparitor and complicated control logic incurring only a 3% performance penalty (Table A.53). The key idea is to generate illegal addresses for the unpredictable but uncommon activation record references, and to guarantee that the common and predictably referenced activation records reside in memory when needed (Section A.5.3).

3.5.3. Virtual Memory

The SOAR system will include disk storage and thus supports virtual memory. Section 5.4 explains our choice of demand paging over segmentation. SOAR therefore includes a pin to request a page fault interrupt. The uniform size and lack of side-effects of SOAR's instructions simplify page fault recovery.

3.6. Implementation

In this section, we give a brief description of SOAR's implementation and microarchitecture. This is covered in more detail in Pendleton's dissertation [Pen85b]. The casual reader may want to skip this section; those interested in details may want to read on and learn about the data path required for SOAR's instruction set. Although simpler than many other computers, SOAR's implementation is substantially more complex than its predecessor, RISC II.

3.6.1. Special Registers

SOAR has eight special-purpose registers that simplify the instruction set and help with interrupt handling (Tables 3.6 and 3.7). For instance, a register that always contains zero permits the assembler to synthesize moves with add instructions. Making the program counter available as a register provides relative addressing without adding another addressing mode. However, supporting unrestricted use of these registers would complicate SOAR. Three restrictions apply to these registers:

- A result written to a special register does not take effect until the end of the next instruction. The SOAR microengine cannot *forward* special registers.

- A special register cannot appear as the destination of a *load* instruction.

- A special register cannot appear in the SOURCE2 field of an instruction.

3.6.2. The SOAR Datapath

The SOAR datapath includes a register file, ALU (and byte shifter), the program counter, memory address register, and saved window pointer. When reading, the busses are first precharged, then two separate registers may be read onto the busses. For writing, a single register is addressed, and the data are driven differentially on both busses (Figure 3.14).

3.6.3. Pipelining in SOAR

The cycle time of SOAR has been matched to memory cycle time. Each instruction is one word long and most can execute in one cycle. While one instruction executes, the next is prefetched from memory (Figure 3.15). As described above, jumps and calls require no address computation and therefore cause no delay in the pipeline. Conditional branches are synthesized with a skip

Table 3.6: SOAR special registers.

Name	Symbol	Reg.	Bits	Contents	Notes
rzero	rzero	r16	31:0	Always = 0.	For synthesizing instructions.
program counter	pc	r17	27:0	address of next instruction	For instruction fetching, PC-relative addressing, and case statement indirect jump *(ret)*. Should not be modified directly, but only with jump, call, or ret[inw].
Shadow A	sha	r19	31:0	copy of A input to ALU or shifter	The shadow registers track instructions executed when interrupts are enabled and freeze when interrupts are disabled. Thus, a trap-handler can save time by reading operand from the shadow registers instead of decoding the offending instruction.
Shadow B	shb	r18	31:0	copy of B input to ALU or shifter	
Trap Base	tb	r21	31:10	base address of the interrupt and trap vector area	
Saved Window Pointer	swp	r20	27:4	memory address of object header of the most recently saved register window	For pointer-to-register logic, window-overflow and -underflow trap logic, and computing address of current activation record. Cwp controls local register decoders.
Current Window Pointer	cwp	r22	6:4	index of on-chip register set serving as **high** window	
Processor Status Word	psw	r23	15:0	see below	

Table 3.7: Processor Status Word fields.			
Name	Bits	Contents	Notes
shadow destination	4:0	destination register field (bits 22:18) of last instruction executed with interrupts enabled	For trap handlers.
software interrupt enable	5	When this bit is on and a call or jump is executed with bit 29 on, SOAR takes a software trap.	For process switching.
interrupt enable	6	Enables I/O interrupts and shadow registers.	Disabled in interrupt handlers.
i	7	inert	Unused.
shadow opcode	15:8	opcode field (bits 30:23) of last instruction executed with interrupts enabled	For trap handlers and trap vector logic. CAVEAT: SOAR does not support nested traps. Traps taken when interrupts are disabled will not vector to proper opcode.

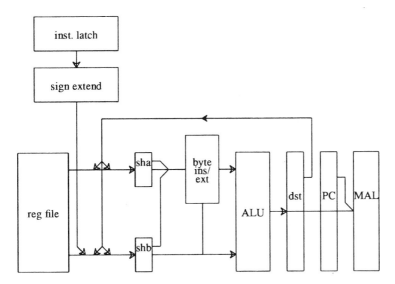

Figure 3.14: The SOAR datapath. "sha" and "shb" are shadow registers A and B, "byte ins/ext" is the byte insertion and extraction logic, "dst" is the destination latch, and "MAL" is the memory address latch.

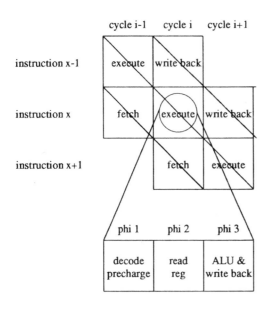

Figure 3.15: Pipelining in SOAR. Although an instruction takes three cycles, SOAR can execute one instruction per cycle. Each cycle in turn consists of three phases.

and an unconditional jump. This takes two cycles, which is the same as a conditional branch would require.

The anatomy of SOAR's cycle is determined by the fact that the datapath allows two simultaneous reads or one write to the register file. Each cycle is divided into three nonoverlapping phases. In phase one, SOAR decodes the instruction and precharges the busses. In phase two, the source registers are read onto the busses. In phase three, the ALU combines the two operands. Simultaneously, the result from the previous instruction is stored back into its destination register. Thus, the result of instruction *i* is not actually stored into its destination register until the end of instruction *i+1*. Forwarding logic hides this delay; if instruction *i+1* attempts to read the destination register of instruction *i*, the desired value is forwarded from a latch at the output of the ALU. This has a significant effect on performance; if instead of forwarding, SOAR stalled the pipeline for a cycle the benchmarks would run 15% slower (Table A.54).

Pendleton has proposed a rearrangement of the pipeline that would shorten SOAR's cycle time by 25% [Pen85b]. However, the return instruction would be one cycle longer, for a total of three cycles per return instruction. What would be the net effect? On the average, SOAR performs 5.4 returns per 100 cycles (Table A.47). Thus, the effect of lengthening the return instruction would be to execute 5.4% more cycles. Since the new cycle time would be 25% faster, the new time to run the benchmarks would be 1.054×75%=79% of the old time. (See Section 4.1 for a description of the benchmarks.) Rearranging SOAR's pipeline would substantially reduce execution time.

3.6.4. Implementation Statistics

Table 3.8 contains some preliminary data for the NMOS SOAR chip, taken from [Pen85b]. These chips were fabricated by MOSIS [MOSIS] and performed faster than the simulators predicted, except for the unforeseen delay for jumps and calls described in Section 3.4.3. The MOSIS NMOS SOAR chips can execute an instruction every 400 ns, which must be derated to 510 ns for the jump and call delay. Pendleton has perfected the host board for SOAR, and has successfully run the entire diagnostic suite on the SOAR chips. The best SOAR chip tested to date functioned perfectly with the exception of a faulty bit in one register.

3.7. Summary

In designing SOAR, we have attempted to find a few good ideas to supplement a basic RISC for Smalltalk. These appear in Table 3.9. As a result of these features, SOAR is considerably more complicated than RISC II. The next chapter evaluates our architecture, and identifies its successes and failures.

Table 3.8: NMOS SOAR characteristics.	
line width	4 μ
size (w/ scribe lines)	
width	10.7 mm
height	8.0 mm
power dissipation	~3 watts
supply voltage	5 volts
transistors	35,700
clocks	
φ1	90 ns
underlap	<10 ns
φ2	90 ns
underlap	<25 ns
φ3	145 ns
underlap	40 ns
processor cycle time	<400 ns
fast shuffle settling time	110 ns
minimum system cycle time	510 ns
actual system cycle time	800 ns
pads	82

Table 3.9: SOAR Architectural Ideas.		
Idea	Section	From
31-bit arithmetic (with tag & overflow checking)	2	
a tagged/untagged mode bit in each instruction	2	
conditional skips	2	PDP-8
tagged immediate values	2	
compilation to low level instruction set	3	RISC II
uniform length instructions	3	RISC II
word-addressing w/ byte-insert and -extract	3	MIPS, PDP-10
instructions tagged as integers	3	
vectored, prioritized interrupts and traps	3	
shadow registers	3	
in-line call target cache	4	Xerox ST-68K
software trap on jumps and traps	4	
one-cycle calls and jumps (fast shuffle)	4	
factored return instruction	4	
parallel register initialization on return	4	
load- and store-multiple	4	IBM-360
multiple overlapping register windows on chip	4	RISC II
noncontiguous load- and store-multiple	4	
generation scavenging	5	
trapping stores of new pointers into old objects	5	BS
trapping stores of activation record pointers	5	BS
trapping returns from referenced activation records	5	
pointers to registers	5	
paged virtual memory	5	Atlas, Sun
direct object addressing	5	BS
special registers	6	RISC II
pipelined data path with forwarding	6	RISC II
offline reorganization		BS
tag checking of addresses for load & store		
hard-wired instructions		RISC II

Chapter 4

Performance Evalutation of the SOAR Architecture

4.1. Introduction

Can a reduced instruction set computer make Smalltalk-80 practical? In this section we evaluate SOAR's overall performance, place it in context with other Smalltalk-80 systems, and examine features in the architecture to see which pull their weight and which are just a waste of effort. Toward this end, we have analyzed running times and instruction mixes of instruction-level simulations of Smalltalk-80 benchmarks (Figure 4.1).

We have instrumented the SOAR simulator to record two types of data: frequencies and profiles. Obtaining data from the simulator makes it possible to measure execution without altering the program being measured. The simulator counts the number of times it executes each instruction, the number of each type of trap taken, and other events. The simulator also samples the program counter every hundred instructions. To gather the data, we run a benchmark once, reset the simulator's counters, enable profiling, run the benchmark for a second iteration and then dump the raw data to files. (Appendix B contains our raw frequency data.) Unix^{TM} utilities *(awk* and *sed)* analyze the data and report the usage and value of particular features. (Appendix A contains these results.)

Xerox has defined an official set of benchmarks for the Smalltalk-80 system [McC83]. Some are called "micro-benchmarks" because they test particular small operations like integer addition. The rest are called "macro-benchmarks" because they test large operations like compilation, display, and exploring system organization. These are typical high-level activities for Smalltalk-80 pro-

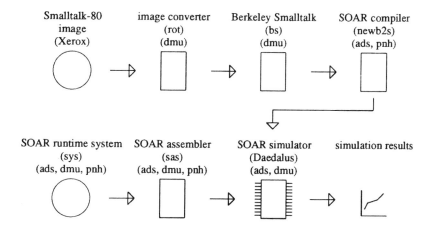

Figure 4.1: Steps involved in a SOAR simulation. First, *rot* removes the object table from the Xerox Smalltalk-80 image. We then use BS to make any modifications necessary in the image (e.g. to eliminate some *becomes*). Newb2s produces a Smalltalk image for SOAR by convert-ing the BS objects to SOAR format, and running Hilfinger's *Slapdash* compiler which translates the bytecoded programs to SOAR instructions. We have also coded the Smalltalk primitive operations and storage management software in SOAR assembly language. After this is assembled, it is fed to *Daedalus*, our SOAR simulator along with the Smalltalk image. The initials below each system indicate its author: ads is Dain Samples, phn is Paul Hilfinger, and dmu is David Ungar.

grammers. We selected five macro-benchmarks for our measurements. When writing Smalltalk-80 programs, we spend more time waiting for the compiler than for anything else. For this reason, we started with the **testCompiler** bench-mark. The other four benchmarks were chosen because they did not output to the display and did not require substantial modifications for SOAR. Although fast display output is vital for Smalltalk, it has been addressed by many others, and is outside the scope of this dissertation. The following descriptions of the benchmarks we chose quote from [McC83]:

testClassOrganizer

"This benchmark measures the speed of conversion between the textual and the structural representations of a class organization. The example chosen is class **Benchmark** because its organization contains many categories.''

testPrintDefinition

''This benchmark measures how quickly a class definition, as it appears in the system browser, can be generated. The example chosen is an instance of class **Compiler** because it has a moderate number of instance variables.''

testPrintHierarchy

''This benchmark times the printing of a portion of the Smalltalk-80 class hierarchy. The example chosen is class **InstructionStream** because it has several subclasses.''

testCompiler

''This benchmark measures the speed of the compiler on a slightly longer than normal method, one containing 87 tokens and compiling into 73 bytecodes.''

testDecompiler

''This benchmark measures the speed of the **Decompiler** by decompiling all the methods in class **InputSensor**.''

In addition, we used a few micro-benchmarks to evaluate an upper bound for the performance impact of specific features:

testPopStoreInstVar

''This benchmark measures how quickly a value can be popped off the stack and stored in an instance variable of the receiver. Because this value is the **SmallInteger** 1, there is little reference counting overhead on the push or store. 50% of the bytes in the block are 16r60,* a pop of the top of the stack into the receiver's first instance variable.''

test3plus4

''This benchmark measures the speed of **SmallInteger** addition. Because all values are **SmallIntegers**, there is little reference-counting overhead. 25% of the bytes in the block are 16rB0,* a quick send of the message +.''

testActivationReturn

"This very important benchmark uses a call on a doubly-recursive method to measure the speed of method activation and return. There is little reference-counting overhead associated with knowing when to end the recursion, but there may be a great deal in managing the **Contexts** that represent the activations. About 12.5% of the bytes executed during this benchmark are 16rE0,* a send of the method's first literal (in this case, the **Symbol recur:**), and about 12.5% are returns, split evenly between 16r78,* a quick return of the receiver, and 16r7C,* a return of the value on the top of the stack.''

How representative are these five macro-benchmarks? Xerox rates the performance of Smalltalk-80 systems relative to the Dorado by taking the mean of the 13 macro-benchmarks plus the text scanning and BitBlt micro-benchmarks [Bay84]. Table 4.1 below compares the compiler benchmark, the median of the five macro-benchmarks used here, and the Xerox performance rating for four other Smalltalk-80 systems. The data suggest that the benchmarks we used slightly underestimate overall performance.

We have not considered the interaction between the availability of hardware features and the sophistication of the optimizations performed by the compiler. The only compiler changes we have taken into account are those required to simulate the missing hardware. For example, to compute the overhead of software type checking, we counted the number of times that hardware type checking was performed by code from the current compiler and multipled that

---

* The 16r prefix denotes a hexadecimal number. For example, 16r7C is 124.

Table 4.1: Comparison of Performance Metrics.			
	compiler	median of classOrganizer compiler decompiler printDefinition printHierarchy	Xerox Performance Rating
Berkeley Smalltalk on Sun 2 [Bay84]	11%	11%	14%
Tektronix 4404 [Bay84]	25%	25%	26%
Xerox PS on Sun 2 [Bay85]	31%	41%	44%
Xerox PS on Sun 3 [Bay85]	80%	99%	109%
Xerox Dorado	100%	100%	100%
SOAR (simulated @ 400 ns)	103%	107%	?

count by the cost of a software check. It is possible that a Smalltalk-80 compiler for a machine without hardware support for type checking would reduce the overhead with a data-flow analysis to eliminate redundant type checking. However, such techniques are not used in existing Smalltalk-80 compilers, which must cope with dynamic type binding. The performance measurements in this dissertation hold only for Smalltalk-80 systems with state-of-the-art compiler technology.

4.2. Overall Performance: SOAR vs Dorado

Can SOAR provide acceptable performance with a single-chip processor? The Dorado is the only Smalltalk-80 system that everyone agrees is fast enough. If SOAR can run as fast as a Dorado, it will certainly provide a usable Smalltalk-80 system. (The Xerox MC68020 Smalltalk-80 system is also approaching the Dorado's performance.) Table 4.2 compares SOAR's performance to the Dorado on five macro-benchmarks and the procedure call micro-benchmark. The Dorado numbers were obtained from Xerox's Smalltalk-80 Newsletter [Bay84]. The SOAR numbers were obtained by simulating the benchmarks for two iterations, taking the number of cycles for the second iteration,* and multiplying by 400 ns†, our measured cycle time for the

4µ chips. These data show that a 400 ns SOAR will perform well enough to please everyone who already uses Smalltalk-80.

4.3. Relative Performance of SOAR

In the previous section, we showed that SOAR will run as fast as a Dorado. How does this compare to other Smalltalk-80 systems? Table 4.3 compares the performance of the compiler benchmark on several Smalltalk-80 systems. Both SOAR and the 68010 are NMOS microprocessors, although the 68010 has almost twice as many transistors as SOAR: 68,000 vs. 35,700. Since Deutsch and Schiffman's ST68K is also a compiled implementation [DeS84], it serves as the fairest architectural comparison to SOAR. Unlike the ST68K code translator,

Table 4.2: SOAR Macro-Benchmark results, relative to Dorado.					
Benchmark	Cycles/iter	# iter	SOAR time (secs)	Dorado time (secs)	SOAR speed relative to Dorado
testActivationReturn	483694	1	0.193	0.996	515%
testClassOrganizer	3206197	1	1.28	1.207	94%
testCompiler	1095039	5	2.19	2.256	103%
testDecompiler	2893596	1	1.16	1.243	107%
testPrintDefinition	74159	20	0.593	0.849	143%
testPrintHierarchy	117585	10	0.470	1.000	213%
min					94%
median					107%
max					213%

---

* We consider the second iteration to be more representative. Had we used the numbers for the first iteration, initial subroutine lookups would have slowed the benchmarks down by up to 10%.

† Implementation problems with the fast shuffle (Section 3.4.3) will prevent full speed operation unless the memory cycle time can be reduced by 100 ns over the chip cycle time. Alternatively, the fast shuffle signal can be ignored, and the chip could run as a delayed branch architecture [Pen85a].

Table 4.3: Compiler Benchmark speed for various Smalltalk-80 systems.
Speed relative to Dorado, larger is faster.

	host processor	instruction time (ns)		execution model	speed
BS	UCB	68010	400	interpreter	11%
Tek 4404	Tektronix	68010	400	interpreter	25%
PS	Xerox	68010	400	compiler	40%
PS	Xerox	68020	180*	compiler	80%
Dorado	Xerox	Dorado	70	microcode	100%
SOAR	UCB	SOAR	400	compiler	103%

the current SOAR compiler generates unnecessary instructions (see Table 2.11); a better compiler would improve SOAR's performance. By creating a custom processor, we have more than doubled performance, while halving the number of transistors.

4.4. Evaluating Individual Features

Although SOAR's design was driven by empirical results, our experimental subject at that time was a bytecode interpreter, not a SOAR simulator. Now that we have a compiler, simulator, and run-time support software for SOAR, we have been able perform an accurate assessment its features (Table 4.4). (Appendix A contains detailed derivations of the data.) Each row gives the feature's name, the minimum, average, and maximum effect it would have on speed were it omitted or added, and the effect it would have on total memory size. For example, the tagged integer support is described in Section 3.2. If left out of SOAR, and if the compiler were unchanged, the macro-benchmarks we simulated would take from 14% to 47% longer to run, with an average time penalty of 26%. The SOAR Smalltalk-80 virtual image would grow by 15% from its 1.5

---

* The cycle time is 180 ns for an instruction that is found in the on-chip cache, and 270 ns for one that is not.

MB. Remember that (except for rearranging the pipeline) our performance figures count cycles and neglect the interaction between architecture and cycle time. For a discussion of cycle time effects, see Pendleton's dissertation [Pen85b].

Table 4.4 groups the features in the order that they were presented in the last chapter. In Table 4.5, we have reordered them by average performance impact and added Pendleton's complexity results in order to identify winner and losers. The complexity index combines the number of diagnostics, circuit blocks, and hand-drawn transistors required for a feature. For example, the most complicated feature, multiple on -chip register windows, has an index of 10.

The importance of register windows on SOAR stems from an important feature of the Smalltalk-80 system, fast compilation. Like some other exploratory programming environments, the Smalltalk-80 system achieves split-second compilation times by compiling each procedure by itself; there are no macros, interprocedural analysis, nor static interprocedural binding. Thus, the compiler runs fast because it has shed the burden of binding or optimizing subroutine calls. This results in a high frequency of subroutine calls, which forces hardware to shoulder the responsibility for efficient execution of calls. This explains why register windows are so effective for SOAR. Although they add the most complexity of any feature [Pen85b], SOAR would run 46% slower without them.

The data suggest that we could simplify SOAR without sacrificing much performance. If we removed all but the winning features, SOAR would only take 19% more time and 8% more memory. Adding Pendleton's pipeline rearrangement would then result in a simpler design with the same performance as the original. If we were to include more features, they might be trap instructions, loadm/storem, and vectored traps. Such a design would be 11% faster than SOAR, and use only 4% more memory.

Table 4.4: Summary of features and performance impacts.

feature	section in book	slowdown if omitted			expansion if omitted*
		best case	average	worst case	
type checking					
tagged integers	3.2.1	14%	26%	47%	15%
two-tone instructions	3.2.3	13%	16%	20%	19%
tagged immediates	3.2.4	7.7%	9.6%	11%	1.2%
interpretation					
compilation	3.3.1	n.a.	100%†	n.a.	-33%
byte ins/ext instructions	3.3.1	2.6%	33%	86%	0
loadc	3.3.1	0.05%	0.46%	1.1%	0
sll	3.3.1	0	0	0	0
trap instructions	3.3.2	3.2%	3.9%	5.2%	2.0%
shadow registers	3.3.2	0.01%	0.04%	0.12%	0
vectored traps	3.3.2	1.7%	2.9%	4.7%	0
fast calls					
register windows	3.4.1	37%	46%	62%	6.1%
loadm/storem	3.4.1	0.59%	3.4%	5.1%	2.0%
in-line cache	3.4.2	27%	33%	40%	-1.2%
fast shuffle	3.4.3	9.6%	11%↑	13%	0
parallel nilling	3.4.4	3.1%	4.3%	6.1%	1.3%
storage management					
generation scavenging	3.5.1	4%	10%	15%	16%‡
direct pointers	3.5.1	15%	22%	29%	2.3%
generation tag hardware	3.5.1	0.25%	1.3%	3.0%	2.9%
pointer-to-register	3.5.1	0.75%	3.1%	7.3%	0
implementation					
forwarding	3.6.3	12%	15%	18%	0
new feature	section in book	speedup if added			compaction if added*
		worst case	average	best case	
compare-and-branch	3.2.2	2.1%	2.6%	3.0%	1.3%
load/store byte	3.3.1	3.6%	7.0%	13%	0
barrel shifter	3.3.1	0.15%	0.37%	0.59%	0
multiply/divide	3.3.1	0.0%	3.2%	8.4%	0
one cycle traps	3.3.2	0.33%	0.63%	1.1%	0
instantaneous call lookup	3.4.2	n.a.	n.a.	23%	1.2%
rearranged pipe [Pen85b]	3.6.3	20%	21%	22%	0

---

* The static measurements were performed on our latest image (Feb. 85). The total size of this image is 1689 kB, however this includes the old bytecoded object code. When those are subtracted out, the image size drops to 1409 kB. Since we do not yet know whether or not we will keep the bytecoded object code, we have chosen to use the (two significant figure) average of 1,500 kB as the image size.

† Rough estimate based on discussion with L. P. Deutsch comparing various Smalltalk-80 implementations.

‡ This row compares Generation Scavenging to Ballard's modified semispaces (see 5.7.2), Deutsch-Bobrow deferred reference counting (see 5.6.2), and immediate reference counting (see 5.6.1), respectively.

↑ Pendleton has discovered that SOAR's implementation of this feature lengthened its cycle time by ~25%.

Table 4.5: Features in order of performance impact.

(Except for rearranged pipeline, excludes impact on cycle time.)

feature	slowdown if omitted	expansion if omitted	complexity [Pen85b]
winners			
compilation	~100%	-33%	0
register windows*	46%	6.1%	10.0
in-line cache	33%	-1.2%	1.3
byte insert/extract instructions	33%	0	4.0
tagged integers†	26%	15%	4.6
direct pointers‡	22%	2.3%	0
two-tone instructions†	16%	19%	n.a.
generation scavenging‡	10%	16%	0
forwarding	15%	0	4.0
fast shuffle↑	11%	0	0.8
tagged immediates†	9.6%	1.2%	0.9
questionable			
parallel nilling	4.3%	1.3%	2.5
trap instructions	3.9%	2.0%	1.7
loadm/storem*	3.4%	2.0%	1.6
pointer-to-register*	3.1%	0	4.4
vectored traps	2.9%	0	1.4
generation tag hardware†	1.3%	2.9%	2.3
losers			
loadc	0.46%	0	0
shadow registers	0.04%	0	3.2
sll	0	0	0

feature	speedup if added	compaction if added	
winners			
call target lookup hardware	<23%	1.2%	
rearranged pipe [Pen85b]	21%	0	
load/store byte	7.0%	0	
losers			
multiply/divide	3.2%	0	
compare-and-branch	2.6%	1.3%	
one cycle traps	0.63%	0	
barrel shifter	0.37%	0	

* Register windows, load- and store-multiple, and pointer-to-register all interact. For example, without register windows, load- and store-multiple would become much more important, and pointer-to-register would be completely silly.

† Tagged integer instructions, two-tone instructions, tagged immediates, and generation tag hardware interactions must be considered. For example, once tagged integer instructions are eliminated, the penalty for eliminating two-tone instructions becomes zero.

‡ The introduction of Generation Scavenging allowed us to exploit direct pointers.

↑ Pendleton has discovered that SOAR's implementation of this feature lengthened the cycle time by ~25%. See Section 3.4.3.

Four of the features in SOAR are mistakes: parallel nilling, pointer-to-register, generation tag hardware, and shadow registers.* Although fully aware of it, we still fell into what we now call the ''architect's trap'' at least four times:

- Each mistake was a clever idea;

- Each made a particular operation much faster;

- Each increased design and simulation time;

- Not one significantly improved overall performance.

Another way to appreciate the worthlessness of these four features is that load/store byte instructions would save more cycles than these four put together.

We have put these results to use by calculating the performance of some variations on SOAR and comparing them to some real systems (Table 4.6). Our predictions of SOAR's performance are based on simulated macro-benchmark times and do not include virtual memory, operating system, and I/O overhead. However, all of the Smalltalk-80 systems we know about tend to be compute-bound for program development. For a fair comparison, we assume a 400 ns cycle time for SOAR, RISC II, and MC68010.

By comparing the speeds of different systems, we can gain some insight into the reasons for SOAR's good performance:

- The speed ratio of full SOAR to RISC II, 1.6 is the same as the ratio of RISC II to the Xerox 68010 system. This indicates that the reduced instruction set architecture (including register windows) and the Smalltalk-specific hardware features contribute equally to performance.

---

* Loadc and sll neither help nor hinder. Calling them mistakes is too perjorative; we would rather think of them as idle pastimes.

Table 4.6: Trimming the Fat from SOAR. *(Assumes 400 ns cycle time for SOAR, RISC II, and 68010)*		
configuration	speed	image size
winners only + rearranged pipeline	103%	108%
full SOAR	100%	100%
Dorado	97%	
winners only	81%	108%
RISC II	62%	126%
full SOAR without software ideas	41%	84%
Xerox 68010 compiler	39%	
full SOAR without hardware ideas	34%*	132%
Tek 68010 interpreter	24%	
stripped SOAR	22%	133%

- Interestingly, the Deutsch-Schiffman 68010 compiled system is a bit better than the estimate for SOAR with only the software ideas. Perhaps the optimizations in Deutsch's compiler account for the difference.

- Since the Tektronix system neither compiles nor scavenges, its software resembles a stripped SOAR. Thus, the similar performance of the Tek system to stripped SOAR suggests that the stripped SOAR hardware performs as well as the MC68010.

The simplicity and high performance of eliminating all but the winning features and rearranging SOAR's pipeline make this an appealing design.

---

* This figure includes an additional 36% time penalty for losing both windows and loadm/storem.

4.5. Conclusions

SOAR's hardware and software design represents an advance for object-oriented experimental programming environments. SOAR has almost half of the transistors of the 68010, yet runs Smalltalk-80 2.5 times faster. Register windows, tagged integer instructions, direct pointers, and generation scavenging account for most of the difference. These four ideas represent SOAR's most important contribution to EPE systems.

Our analysis of a feature's value was based on counting cycles. Barring the pipeline rearrangement, we ignored the effect of adding a feature on the cycle time (see [Pen85b]). In fact, some of the features we added to the machine must have perversely increased the cycle time enough to offset the reduction in cycles, thereby slowing down the system. In particular, the hardware support for automatic storage reclamation probably did not speed up SOAR. Other examples of mistakes in SOAR are the inclusion of parallel register nilling, logic to support pointers to registers, and shadow registers to aid trap handling. We observe that the inclusion of interesting features that complicate the design but do not improve the performance of *representative* programs is a trap that many architects fall prey to, including us.*

There are four places to look for further performance gains: compiler technology (outside the scope of this dissertation), implementation technology (see [Pen85b]), optimization of the run-time support primitives (which consume about two thirds of SOAR's time), and better hardware or software algorithms to cache call target lookups (which consume 23% of SOAR's time). Of these, im-

---

* Pendleton has discovered that SOAR's implementation of the Fast Shuffle incurs a 25% penalty when the chip is used with a 400 ns memory system (Section 3.4.3). This dwarfs the architectural benefit of an 11% reducion in the number of cycles. In this case the culprit was our failure to simulate the memory system along with chip.

plementation technology — circuit design and VLSI processing technology — have the most dramatic impact. Since we started this project, the standard VLSI technology available to universities has improved from 4μ line widths to 3μ. This one change should reduce our cycle time from 400 ns to 290 ns, as important a contribution as register windows. Another example is Pendleton's pipeline rearrangement which could improve performance by 21%. This is more than the combined effect of parallel nilling, trap instructions, loadm/storem, pointer-to-register, vectored traps, and generation tag-checking hardware.

A 70 ns ECL Dorado is the only existing machine that runs Smalltalk-80 fast enough to satisfy everyone, and the 400 ns NMOS SOAR chips that have been fabricated should run just as fast. Thus, SOAR will support the Smalltalk-80 system with excellent performance.

Chapter 5

Non-Disruptive High Performance Storage Reclamation

Throw back the little ones
and pan fry the big ones;
use tact, poise and reason
and gently squeeze them.
              Steely Dan, ''Throw Back the Little Ones'' [BeF74]

5.1. Introduction

Early in the SOAR project, we realized that automatic storage reclamation could easily become a bottleneck. We knew the overhead for allocation and freeing in Smalltalk-80 systems ranged from 10% to 15% [DeS84, UnP83], that some reclamation algorithms introduced annoying pauses, that some required the programmer to explicitly free circular structures of objects, and that most of the algorithms required microcode support. Since we needed to attain good performance in a system without microcode we have designed, implemented, and measured *Generation Scavenging*, a new garbage collector that

- limits pause times to a fraction of a second,

- requires no hardware support,

- meshes well with virtual memory,

- reclaims circular structures, and

- uses only 3% of the CPU time in SOAR. This is less than a third of the time of deferred reference counting, the next best algorithm.*

---

* Experience with SOAR has made us realize that some of the other algorithms that are usually microcoded need not be. Although our original reason for searching for a new algorithm proved to be unfounded, we found something that enjoys solid advantages in performance and the ability to reclaim circular structures.

This section describes the challenge of providing automatic storage reclamation, surveys some popular algorithms, and presents our solution. It concludes by evaluating the performance of Generation Scavenging, based on running the Smalltalk-80 benchmarks [McC83] on BS and simulating them on SOAR. An earlier and shorter version of this chapter appeared in [Ung84].

5.2. The Relationship Between Virtual Memory and Storage Reclamation

The storage manager must ensure an ample supply of virtual addresses for new objects, and must maintain a working set of existing objects in physical memory. Traditionally, the functions have been separated into two parts as shown in Table 5.1 and Figure 5.1.

Sometimes the distinction between virtual memory and automatic reclamation can lead to inefficiency or redundant functionality. For example, some garbage collection (GC) algorithms require that an object be in main memory when

Table 5.1: Traditional decomposition of storage management.		
name	responsibility	pitfall
virtual memory	fetching data from disk	thrashing
auto reclamation	recycling address space	distracting pauses to GC

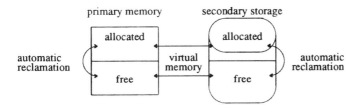

Figure 5.1: Virtual memory vs. automatic storage reclamation.

it is freed; this may cause extra backing store operations. As another example, both compaction and virtual memory make room for new objects by moving old ones. Thus storage reclamation algorithms and virtual memory strategies must be designed to accommodate each other's needs.

5.3. Personal Computers Must Be Responsive

Personal computers differ from time-sharing systems. For example, with personal computers there are no other users to blame for distracting pauses. Yet personal machines have time available for periodic offline tasks, for even the most fanatic hackers sleep occasionally. Personal computers promise consistently short response times which are known to boost productivity significantly [Tha81].

5.4. Virtual Memory for Advanced Personal Computers

Computers with fast, random access secondary storage can exploit program locality to manage main memory for the programmer. Advanced personal computer systems manage memory in many small chunks, or objects. The Symbolics ZLISP, Cedar-Mesa, Smalltalk-80, and Interlisp-D systems are examples. Table 5.2 summarizes segmentation and paging, the two virtual memory techniques.

5.4.1. Segmentation

A segmented virtual memory enjoys the flexibility of placing each object in physical memory independently of the other objects. This packing efficiency can result in better use of main memory and a reduction in time-consuming backing store operations. However, segmentation's performance advantage disappears when main memory becomes more plentiful [Sta82, Sta84]. Moreover, the variety and quantity of objects in advanced personal computer systems

Table 5.2: Segmentation vs. Paging.		
	segmentation	paging
chunk size (bytes)	16 to 65,384	512, 1024, 2048, or 4096
# address space subdivisions	8 - 65,384	128 - 65,384
translation map	associative	direct or associative
space overhead	disk buffers	unused portions of pages
time overhead	copying from buffers	offline reorganization*
first implemented	B 5000 (1961)[LoK61]	Atlas (1962)[KEL62]
current example	Intel iAPX-286	VAX-11

pose tough challenges for a segmented virtual memory. In our Smalltalk-80 memory image, for example, the length of an object can vary from 24 bytes (points), to 128,000 bytes (bitmaps), with a mean of about 50. Suppose segmentation alone is used. When an object is created or swapped in, a piece of main memory as large as the object must be found to hold it. Thus, a few large bitmaps can crowd out many smaller but more frequently referenced objects.

When objects are small, it takes many of them to accomplish anything. Smalltalk-80 systems already contain 32,000 to 64,000 objects, and this number is increasing. A segmented memory with this many segments requires either a prohibitively large or a content-addressable segment table.[†] This large number hampers address translation.

5.4.2. Demand Paging

The simplicity of page table hardware and the opportunity to hide the address translation time make paging attractive to hardware designers [Den70].

---

* While BS is the first paging Smalltalk system to employ offline reorganization of the virtual space [Bla83d], object swapping systems starting with OOZE did reorganizations regularly [Ing83].

† The OOZE virtual memory system for Smalltalk-76 solved this problem but incurred other costs: it was limitied to 65K objects, the object table required a hash probe for every object access, and a disk access was needed to create a new temporary object if its pointer was on a free list [Ing83].

Paging, however, is not a panacea for advanced personal computers. It can squander main memory by dispersing frequently referenced small objects over many pages. Blau has shown that periodic offline reorganization can prevent this disaster [Bla83d]. The daily idle time of a personal computer can be used to repack objects onto pages.

Many objects in advanced personal computers live only a short time. The paging literature contains little about strategies for such objects. Since their lifetimes are shorter than the time to access backing store, these objects should never be paged out. By segregating short-lived objects from permanent ones, Generation Scavenging permits them to be locked in main memory. Table 5.3 summarizes the obstacles that advanced personal computers pose for a paged virtual memory, and the solutions that SOAR has adopted. BS and the DEC VAX/Smalltalk-80 system [BaS83] use paging.

5.5. Automatic Storage Reclamation for Advanced Personal Computers

Advanced personal computers depend on efficient automatic storage reclamation. For example, Berkeley Smalltalk allocates a new object every 80 instructions. This is consistent with Foderaro's results for a few voracious Lisp programs [FoF81]. Since the total size of the system was in an equilibrium for these measurements, the reclamation rate must match the allocation rate. The

Table 5.3: Paging problems and solutions.		
problem	description	SOAR solution
internal fragmentation	1 object per page	offline reorganization
address size	need 64K 50 byte objects	big addresses (2^{28} words)
paging short-lived objects	page faults for dead objects	segregation by age, don't page new ones

mean dynamic object size is 70 bytes long. Thus, seven bits must be reclaimed for every instruction executed.

Let's examine several garbage collection algorithms and evaluate their suitability for advanced personal computers. Where possible, we use performance figures from actual implementations of these algorithms. The Xerox Dorado Smalltalk-80 system is closest to an advanced personal computer; when we try to compare results we shall normalize to that speed. For example, the bandwidth imposed on the BS storage allocator is

$$\frac{70 \; bytes}{1 \; object} \times \frac{1 \; object}{80 \; instructions} \times \frac{9000 \; bytecodes}{second} = 7800 \; \frac{bytes}{second}.$$

If we scale this up to the speed of the Xerox Dorado system, the storage allocation rate exceeds 100 KB/s.

Jon L. White was one of the first researchers to exploit the overlap between the functions of virtual memory and garbage collection, and he proposed that address space reclamation was obsolete in a virtual memory system [Whi80]. He pointed out that as long as referenced objects were compacted into main memory, dead objects would be paged out to backing store. This strategy may have adequate performance as far as CPU time and main memory utilization, but it demands too much from the backing store in a Smalltalk-80 system. Even if a 100 MB backing store could keep up with the 100 KB/sec allocation bandwidth it would fill up in less than an hour:

$$\frac{100MB \; / \; disk}{100KB \; trash \; / \; second} \approx 20 \; minutes.$$

This is unacceptable.

There are many automatic storage reclamation algorithms [Coh81], but they can be divided into two families: those that maintain reference counts and those that traverse and mark live objects. In the next few sections, we examine several reclamation algorithms and discuss their suitability for advanced personal computers.

5.6. Reclaiming Storage by Counting References

Reference counting was invented in 1960 [Col60] and has undergone many refinements [Knu73, Sta80]. The central idea is to maintain a count of the pointers that reference each object. If an object's reference count should fall to zero, the object is no longer accessible and its space can be reclaimed (Figure 5.2).

5.6.1. Immediate Reference Counting

Immediate reference counting adjusts reference counts on every store instruction and reclaims an object as soon as its count drops to zero. Both the Dorado Smalltalk-80 system [GoR83] and LOOM [KaK83, Sta82, Sta84] reclaim space with this algorithm. Compaction is handled separately and typically causes a pause of 1.3 seconds every 1 to 20 minutes on a Sun 68010 workstation.

Counting references takes time. For each store, the old contents of the cell must be read so that its referent's count can be decremented, and the new content's referent's count must be increased. This consumes 15% of the CPU time [Deu83b, UnP83]. When an object's count diminishes to zero, the object must be scanned to decrement the counts of everything it references. This *recursive freeing* consumes an additional 5% of execution time [Deu82a, UnP83]. Thus, the total overhead for reference counting is about 20%. This substantial overhead is acceptable for personal computers, but deferred reference counting and Generation Scavenging (discussed below) use much less.

Reference counting cannot reclaim cycles of unreachable objects. Even though the whole cycle is unreachable, each object in it has a non-zero count. Deutsch [Deu83b] believes that this limitation has hurt programming style on the

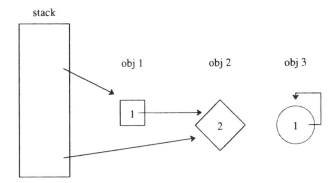

Figure 5.2: Standard reference counting. The standard reference counting algorithm associates a reference count with each object. An object is reclaimed when the count goes to zero. Object 3 is referenced only by itself, and is thus garbage. Since its count is nonzero, it cannot be reclaimed by a reference counting algorithm.

Xerox Smalltalk-80 system (which employs reference counts), and Lieberman [LiH83] has also stated that circular structures are becoming increasingly important for artificial intelligence applications. The advantage of immediate reference counting is that it uses the least amount of memory for temporary objects — about 15 KB when running the Smalltalk-80 macro benchmarks. However, its inability to reclaim circular structures remains a serious drawback for advanced personal computers.

5.6.2. Deferred Reference Counting

The Deutsch-Bobrow deferred reference counting algorithm reduces the cost of maintaining reference counts [DeB76]. Three contemporary personal computer programming environments use this algorithm: Cedar Mesa, InterLisp-D (both on Dorados), and an experimental Smalltalk-80 system which furnished the performance measurements quoted herein [DeS84]. The Deutsch-Bobrow algorithm diminishes the time spent adjusting reference counts by ignoring references from local variables (Figure 5.3). These uncounted references preclude reclamation during program execution. To free dead objects, the system periodically stops, and reconciles the counts with the uncounted references. On a typical personal computer the algorithm requires 25 kB more space than immediate reference counting, and averages 30 ms pauses every 500 ms.

Baden's measurements of a Smalltalk-80 system suggest that this method saves 90% of the reference count manipulation needed for immediate reference counting [Bad82]. Deferred reference counting spends about 3% of the total CPU time manipulating reference counts, 3% for periodic reconciliation, and 5% for recursive freeing. Thus, deferred reference counting uses about half the time of simple reference counting.

What would be the space cost for deferred reference counting on SOAR? The most efficient representation of a reference count on SOAR would be one word per count. Table 5.4 shows the code sequence for reference counting on SOAR. Since this sequence is nine words long, we can multiply the number of tagged stores by nine to compute the code overhead for reference counting on

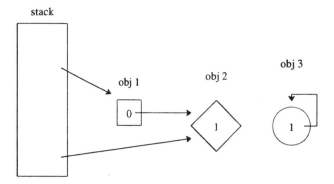

Figure 5.3: Deferred reference counting. The deferred reference counting algorithm does not count references to objects from the execution stack. A zero count does not ensure that an object is reclaimable; it may still have references from the stack.

Table 5.4: Reference counting sequence on SOAR.		
%load	(storeObj)offset, oldContents	
load	(oldContents)countOffset, oldRC	/* tag trap handles int case */
%skip	eq oldRC, 1	
%call	freeRoutine	
%sub	oldRC, 1, oldRC	
%store	oldRC, (oldContents)countOffset	
load	(newContents)countOffset, newRC	
%add	newRC, 1, newRC	
%store	newRC, (newContents)countOffset	

SOAR (Table 5.5). This calculation shows that a straightforward implementation of deferred reference counting would increase the image size by 16%.*

Although more efficient than immediate reference counting, deferred reference counting still does not reclaim circular structures. This is its biggest drawback.

Table 5.5: Static cost for reference counting on SOAR.	
number of tagged store instructions	3578
mean object length	14 words
total size of image	1,500 kB
relative space cost of code	8.59%
relative space cost of counts	7.14%
total space cost	15.73%

---

* The time required to manipulate reference counts on stores is the time to adjust a count, perhaps 25 cycles, times the frequency of tagged store instructions, or 0.36% (Table A.47), divided by the average cycles per instruction, or 1.5. This gives an estimate of 6%. If reconciliation adds another 2%, we obtain a total of 8%, which is consistent with Deutsch's measurements.

5.7. Reclaiming Storage by Finding Reachable Objects

Marking reclamation algorithms collect garbage by first traversing and marking reachable objects and then reclaiming the space filled by unmarked objects. Unlike reference counting, these algorithms reclaim circular structures.

5.7.1. Mark and Sweep

The first marking storage reclamation algorithm, mark and sweep, was introduced in 1960 [McC60]. It has many variations [Coh81, Knu73, Sta80], and is used in contemporary systems [FoF81]. After marking reachable objects, the mark and sweep algorithms reclaim one object at a time, by sweeping the entire address space. Fateman has found that some Franz Lisp programs spend 25% to 40% of their time marking and sweeping [Fat83] and require about 1.9 mB for dynamic objects (compared to about 1 mB for static objects). These algorithms are inefficient because they access a large number of objects; the marking phase inspects all live objects, and the sweeping phase modifies all dead ones.

The marking phase inspects every live object and thereby causes backing store operations.* Foderaro found that for some LISP programs, hints to the virtual memory system could reduce the number of page faults for a mark and sweep from 120 to 90 [FoF81]. Even with hints, marking and sweeping with paging causes on average a 4.5 second pause every 79 seconds. This is unacceptable for an interactive personal computer.

_____

* The sweep phase also requires backing store operations, but its sequential nature accommodates prefetching.

5.7.2. Scavenging Live Objects

The costly phase of sweeping dead objects can be eliminated by moving the live objects to a new area, a technique called *scavenging*. A scavenge is a breadth-first traversal of reachable objects. After a scavenge, the former area is free, so that new objects can be allocated from its base. In addition to the performance savings, a scavenging reclaimer also compacts, obviating a separate compaction pass. Scavenging algorithms must also update pointers to the relocated objects.

Automatic storage reclamation algorithms that scavenge include Baker's semispace algorithm [Bak77], Ballard's algorithm [BaS83], Generation Garbage Collection [LiH83], and Generation Scavenging. Baker's algorithm divides memory into two spaces and scavenges all reachable objects from one space to the other (Figure 5.4). Ballard implemented this algorithm for his VAX/Smalltalk-80 system and observed that many objects were long-lived. The addition of a separate area for these objects resulted in a substantial performance improvement by eliminating the periodic copy of them. Ballard's system has 600 KB for static objects, a 512 KB object table, and two 1 MB semispaces for dynamic objects. It spends only 7% of its time reclaiming storage, including

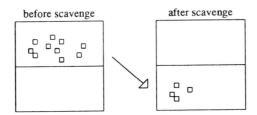

Figure 5.4: Baker semispaces. The Baker storage reclamation algorithm divides memory into semispaces. When one fills up, the live objects in it are copied to the other semispace.

sweeping the object table to reclaim entries. Since it is embedded in an interpretive system that runs Smalltalk-80 programs a twelfth as fast as the Dorado (Table 2.2), the CPU overhead for this algorithm may rise above 7% on a high-performance system.

Generation Garbage Collection [LiH83] exploits the observation that many young objects die quickly and generalizes Baker's algorithm by segregating objects into generations, each within its own space (Figure 5.5). Each generation may be scavenged without disturbing older ones, permitting younger generations to be scavenged more often. This reduces the time spent scavenging older, more stable objects. At present, there are no published performance data on this algorithm.

The scavenging algorithms above incur hidden costs because they interleave scavenging with program execution. The key idea is to avoid pauses due to scavenging by subdividing the work and scavenging a few objects every time a new one is allocated. The problem with mixing execution with reclamation is that the program may try to use a pointer to an object that has been scavenged to another area. This problem can be solved by checking all loads and following the forwarding pointers, but the solution in turn imposes additional overhead on the running program. Thus, eliminating pauses slows execution.

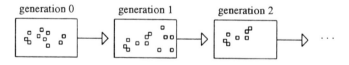

Figure 5.5: Generation garbage collection. Generation garbage collection is a generalization of Baker semispaces. This algorithm divides memory into many small semispaces, one per "generation." When a semispace fills up, its contents are scavenged to the next one.

Algorithms that segregate objects into generations must maintain tables of references from older to younger objects. These algorithms save time by reclaiming space in younger generations without traversing older generations. The burden of maintaining these tables falls on some store instructions.

5.8. The Generation Scavenging Automatic Storage Reclamation Algorithm

Generation Scavenging arose from our attempts find an efficient, unobtrusive storage reclamation algorithm for SOAR that did not require microcode. Our test vehicle was Berkeley Smalltalk, which originally used reference counting. Measurements of BS object lifetimes proved that young objects die young and old objects continue to live. We then designed Generation Scavenging to exploit that behavior and substituted it for reference counting in Berkeley Smalltalk. The result was an eight-fold reduction in the percentage of time spent reclaiming storage — from 13% to 1.5%. In addition, the intrinsic compaction provided by scavenging made it possible to eliminate the Object Table and its accompanying indirection. After eliminating the object table and reference counting, BS ran 1.7 times faster than before. In addition to the performance improvement, since Generation Scavenging was not based on reference counting, it was able to reclaim cycles of unreachable data structures.

5.8.1. Overview of Generation Scavenging Algorithm

Each object is classified as either *new* or *old*. Old objects reside in a region of memory called the *old area*. All old objects that reference new ones are members of the *remembered set*. Objects are added to this set as a side effect of store instructions. (This checking is not required for stores into local variables because stack frames are always new.) Objects that no longer refer to new objects are deleted from the *remembered set* during scavenging. All new objects that are referenced must be reachable directly from the old objects in the *remembered set*, or through a chain of new objects ultimately linked to the *remembered set*. Thus, a traversal in new space, starting at the *remembered set* (and virtual machine registers) can find all live new objects. Table 5.6 summarizes the characteristics of the two generations for Generation Scavenging.

There are three areas for new objects (Figure 5.6):

- *NewSpace*, a large area where new objects are created,

- *PastSurvivorSpace*, which holds new objects that have survived previous scavenges, and

- *FutureSurvivorSpace*, which is used only during scavenging.

A scavenge moves live new objects from NewSpace and PastSurvivorSpace to FutureSurvivorSpace, then interchanges Past and FutureSurvivorSpace. At this point, no live objects are left in NewSpace, and it can be reused to create more objects. The scavenge incurs a space cost of only one bit per object. Its time cost is proportional to the number of live new objects and thus is small since only 1 in 20 objects survive a scavenge. If a new object survives enough scavenges, it moves to the old object area and is no longer subject to online au-

Table 5.6: Generations in Generation Scavenging for BS.		
contents	volatile objects	permanent objects
residence	new space	old space
space size	200 KB*	940 KB
location	main memory	demand paged
created by	instantiation	tenuring
reclaimed by	scavenging	mark-and-sweep
reclaimed every	16 sec	3 - 8 hrs
reclamation takes	0.16 sec	5 min

---

* 140 KB for New area + 2 * 28KB for survivors

tomatic reclamation. This promotion to old status is called *tenuring*. Figure 5.7 depicts both the old and new areas for Generation Scavenging.

5.8.2. Detailed Description of Generation Scavenging

Recall that the purpose of a scavenge is to transport the surviving new objects from NewSpace and PastSurvivorSpace to FutureSurvivorSpace. A one-pass breadth-first algorithm copies the objects and updates pointers to them as it goes along. It starts by searching all the old objects in the *Remembered set* for pointers to new objects, which it copies to FutureSurvivorSpace. Then, it updates the pointer to point to the copy instead of the original, leaves another pointer to the copy in the first word of the original, and sets a flag bit to indicate that the original has been moved. If the scavenging algorithm encounters a reference to the same object again, the flag bit and forwarding pointer will enable it to detect that the object has already been scavenged and to update the

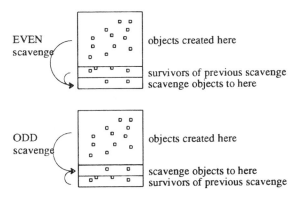

Figure 5.6: Generation Scavenging's three areas for new objects. The largest area holds newly-created objects *(NewSpace)*. Two smaller areas alternately hold objects that have survived previous scavenges *(PastSurvivorSpace)* and receive objects copied by the current scavenge *(FutureSurvivorSpace)*. This unbalanced division saves memory over a semispace algorithm.

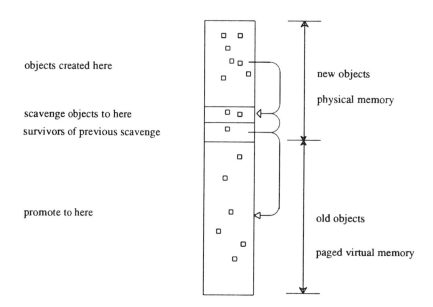

objects created here

new objects

physical memory

scavenge objects to here

survivors of previous scavenge

promote to here

old objects

paged virtual memory

Figure 5.7: Bird's eye view of Generation Scavenging. After an object has survived enough scavenges, it is promoted to the old object area. New objects are locked down in physical memory; old objects reside in virtual memory and may be paged out.

reference. After this first pass, all new objects referenced by old object have been scavenged. Now, the algorithm starts traversing FutureSurvivorSpace and scavenging any new objects referenced from there. As more objects are copied, the end of FutureSurvivorSpace grows away from the scan, until finally, all live new objects have been scavenged and the scan catches up to the end. At this point, the algorithm terminates.

In addition to preserving live objects, those objects that survive for a long time must be promoted into OldSpace. If they were not, much time would be wasted copying and recopying the same objects back and forth. So, each object includes a count of the number of scavenges it has survived. If this count should reach a certain threshold, the object gets scavenged to OldSpace instead of FutureSurvivorSpace. At this point, the object must be added on to the end of the *remembered set* in case it contains any pointers to other new objects. After completing a pass, the algorithm checks the *remembered set*. If it has grown, the new part is scanned, which may add objects to the end of FutureSurvivorSpace. Then, if FutureSurvivorSpace has grown, the new portion of that area must be scanned, which may add objects to the end of the *remembered set*. The final form of the algorithm, therefore resembles two coroutines: one which searches the *remembered set*, and another which searches FutureSurvivorSpace for pointers to new objects. This is easily implemented in C with two subroutines called alternately in a loop. The loop terminates when one of the subroutines completes without adding more objects for the other one to scan.

We now present the Generation Scavenging algorithm top-down, in pidgin C:

```
struct   space {
         word_t *firstWord;      /* start of space */
         int     size;           /* number of used words in space */
};

struct   object {
         int     size,
                 age;
         boolean isForwarded,
                 isRemembered;
         union {
                 struct object   *contents[],
                                 *forwardingPointer;
         };
};


struct space     NewSpace, PastSurvivorSpace, FutureSurvivorSpace, OldSpace;

struct object    *RememberedSetContents[MaxRemembered];
int              RememberedSetSize;
```

```
/*
 *      The main routine, generationScavenge, first scavenges the new
 *      objects immediately reachable from old ones.  Then it scavenges
 *      those that are transitively reachable.  If thus results in
 *      a promotion, the promotee gets remembered, and it first
 *      scavenges objects adjacent to the promotee, then scavenges the
 *      ones reachable from the promoted.  This loop continues until
 *      no more reachable objects are left.  At that point,
 *      PastSurvivorSpace is exchanged with FutureSurvivorSpace.
 *
 *      Notice that each pointer in a live object is inspected once and
 *      only once.  The previousRememberedSetSize and
 *      previousFutureSurvivorSpaceSize variables ensure that no object
 *      is scanned twice, as well as detecting closure.  If this were
 *      not true, some pointers might get forwarded twice.
 */

generationScavenge()
{
        int     previousRememberedSetSize    = 0;
        int     previousFutureSurvivorSpaceSize      = 0;

        while (TRUE) {
                scavengeRememberedSetStartingAt(previousRememberedSetSize);
                if (previousFutureSurvivorSpaceSize == FutureSurvivorSpace.size)
                        break;

                previousRememberedSetSize = RememberedSetSize;
                scavengeFutureSurvSpaceStartingAt(
                   previousFutureSurvivorSpace.size);
                if (previousRememberedSetSize == RememberedSetSize)
                        break;

                previousFutureSurvivorSpaceSize = FutureSurvivorSpace.size;
        }
        exchange(PastSurvivorSpace, FutureSurvivorSpace);
}
```

```
/*
 *      scavengeRememberedSetStartingAt(n) traverses objects in the remembered
 *      set starting at the nth one.  If the object does not refer to any new
 *      objects, it is removed from the set.  Otherwise, its new referents
 *      are scavenged.
 */

scavengeRememberedSetStartingAt(dest)
int dest;
{
        int source;

        for (source = dest;  source < RememberedSetSize;  ++source)
                if (scavengeReferentsOf(RememberedSet[source])) {
                        RememberedSetContents[dest++] =
                                RememberedSetContents[source];
                }
                else
                        resetRememberedFlag(RememberedSetContents[source]);
        RememberedSetSize = dest;

}
```

```
/*
 *      scavengeFutureSurvSpaceStartingAt(n) does a depth-first
 *      traversal of the new objects starting at the one at the nth word
 *      of FutureSurvivorSpace.
 */

scavengeFutureSurvSpaceStartingAt(n)
int n;
{
        struct object *currentObject;

        while (n < FutureSurvivorSpace.size) {
                scavengeReferentsOf(
                   currentObject = FutureSurvivorSpace.firstWord[n]);
                n += sizeOfObject(currentObject))
        }
}
```

```
/*
 *      scavengeReferentsOf(anObject) inspects all the pointers in anObject.
 *      If any are new objects, it has them moved to FutureSurvivorSpace,
 *      and returns truth.  If there are no new referents, it returns falsity.
 *      For simplicity here, an object is just an array of pointers.
 */

scavengeReferentsOf(anObject)
struct object *anObject;
{
        int i;
        boolean foundNewReferrent;
        struct object *referent;

        foundNewReferent = FALSE;
        for (i = 0;  i < anObject->size;  i++) {
                referrent = anObject.contents[i];
                if (isNew(referrent)) {
                        foundNewReferrent = TRUE;
                        if (!isForwarded(referrent))
                                copyAndForwardObject(referent);
                        anObject.contents[i] = referent->forwardingPointer;
                }
        }
        return (foundNewReferrent);
}



/*
 *      copyAndForwardObject(obj) copies a new object either to
 *      FutureSurvivorSpace, or if it is to be promoted, to OldSpace.
 *      It leaves a forwarding pointer behind.
 */

copyAndForwardObject(oldLocation)
struct object *oldLocation;
{
        struct object *newLocation;

        if (oldLocation->obj_age < MaxAge) {
                ++oldLocation->obj_age;
                newLocation = copyObjectToSpace(oldLocation,
                    FutureSurvivorSpace);
        }
        else
                newLocation = copyObjectToSpace(oldLocation, OldSpace);

        oldLocation->obj_forwardingPointer = newLocation;
        oldLocation->obj_forwarded == TRUE;
}
```

How do old objects get reclaimed? An offline reclamation program traverses and copies all objects in depth-first order to a file. This is a three-pass algorithm: The first pass copies the live objects to a file and leaves forwarding pointers in the original objects. The second pass traverses the file and updates the pointers. The third pass reads the file into memory, overwriting the original area. Copying rearranges the objects into depth-first order, which helps to reduce the number of page faults [Bla83b, Bla83d, Sta82, Sta84]. The whole process takes a few minutes. If it is only required once or twice a day, it should not be too disruptive.

5.8.3. Comparing Generation Scavenging to Other Scavenging Algorithms

Generation Scavenging most resembles Ballard's scheme [BaS83]:

- It segregates objects into young and old generations.

- It copies live objects instead of sweeping dead objects.

- It reclaims old objects offline.

Generation Scavenging differs from Ballard's Semispaces and Lieberman-Hewitt's Generation Garbage Collection [LiH83]. Unlike those algorithms, Generation Scavenging

- conserves main memory by dividing new space into three spaces instead of two.

- is not incremental. Instead, the small pauses introduced by Generation Scavenging are unnoticeable in normal interactive sessions. (They are noticeable in real-time applications such as animation.) Incremental algorithms require checking on every load instruction, and Generation Scavenging saves this time by not being incremental.

5.9. Performance Evaluation of Generation Scavenging

How well does Generation Scavenging perform in Berkeley Smalltalk and SOAR? We concentrate on four metrics:

- *CPU time overhead,* the CPU time spent reclaiming storage divided by the total CPU time in the session,

- *pause time,* the time that the user must wait for reclamation,

- *peak main memory usage,* the amount of main memory that must be dedicated for temporary objects, and

- *backing store accesses,* the number of times that the reclamation algorithm requires data not present in main memory.

5.9.1. Evaluating Generation Scavenging in Berkeley Smalltalk

The Smalltalk-80 macro benchmarks [McC83] consist of representative activities like compiling and text editing. We measured the performance of Generation Scavenging in BS while running these benchmarks. Although our workstation had 2 MB of main memory, only about half of that was available to Berkeley Smalltalk. Table 5.7 shows the results.

CPU Time Cost. Our measurements of BS show that Generation Scavenging requires only 1.5% of the total (user CPU) time. This is four times better than its nearest competitor, Ballard's modified semispaces, which takes about 7%.

One reason that Generation Scavenging looks so good is that BS executes programs more slowly than some other Smalltalk-80 systems. However, the next section shows that Generation Scavenging performs well on fast Smalltalk-80 systems.

Table 5.7: Performance of Generation Scavenging in BS.	
total instructions executed	4500 k
amount of storage reclaimed	3900 KB
amount of tenured storage	9.1 KB
number of checked stores	190 k
number of remembered objects	320
number of scavenges	32
mean length of survivors	4.8 Kword
total user CPU time	280 secs.
total Real time	500 secs.
real time scavenging	1.8%
user time scavenging	1.5%
time checking stores	0.1%
max old space used	940 KB
max new space	140 KB
max survivor space	28 KB
total size	1800 KB
resident set size	930 KB
total page faults	61
min pause time*	90 ms
median pause time*	150 ms
mean pause time*	160 ms
90th %ile pause time*	220 ms
max pause time*	330 ms
mean time between scavenges	16 seconds

Main Memory Consumption. Although each of the three new object areas occupies 140 KB of virtual memory (420 KB total), only 28 KB of each survivor area gets used. The rest serves as a reserve against pathological survival and need not be resident. Thus, the total primary memory cost for dynamic objects is 200 KB, about 10% of the BS main memory. If we used Baker semispaces with

---

* excluding first six scavenges, which thrashed because Unix would not let us lock down the new area.

the same scavenging rate, each space would need to be 140KB + 28KB, for a total of 360 KB, almost twice as much as Generation Scavenging.

Backing Store Operations. Since new objects are always created in the same area, they can remain in main memory. Unfortunately, Unix on the Sun 68010 workstation (Sun Release 2.0) does not implement the system call that would lock down this area. Thus, the first six scavenges caused 283 minor page faults (page reclaims), and the rest of the scavenges caused four. With a working set of 930 KB, 60 major page faults occurred during the benchmarks.

Pauses. Except for the page faulting during the first six scavenges (see above), the pauses were small and mostly unobtrusive, averaging 150 ms. The longest pause was only 330 ms. About 15% of the pause time was spent in the Unix kernel on unrelated overhead. Since people have difficulty noticing pauses of 100 ms, this algorithm's performance meets our requirements.

5.9.2. Evaluating Generation Scavenging on SOAR

The previous section shows that Generation Scavenging performs well in BS, requiring fewer than 1.5% of the CPU cycles. How well will this algorithm perform on SOAR? SOAR will run Smalltalk programs ten times faster than BS. This will result in ten times more garbage created in the same amount of time, but, we would not expect Generation Scavenging to run ten times faster on SOAR than in Berkeley Smalltalk. If it ran at the same speed, then the overhead for scavenging on SOAR would be ten times worse, or 15%. In fact, as we show in Section 5.9, Generation Scavenging takes only about 2% of SOAR's time.

5.9.2.1. SOAR Scavenge Duration

We have written Generation Scavenging in SOAR assembly language and simulated it in the course of running the macro benchmarks. Table 5.8 gives measurements of 12 scavenges, 9 from the decompiler benchmark, two from the printDefinition benchmark, and one from the compiler benchmark. (See Chapter 4.1 for a description of the benchmarks.) As expected, the duration of a scavenge can be predicted from the number of words of new objects that survive the scavenge. Figure 5.8 superimposes the observed data with a linear regression. The regression predicts that the number of cycles for a scavenge is $24 \times surviving$ -$words$ +3500 with a correlation coefficient r of 0.976.

The last column of Table 5.8 gives the duration, or pause time of each scavenge, assuming 400 ns per cycle. Despite identical cycle times, SOAR's

| **Table 5.8: Statistics on twelve scavenges simulated for SOAR.** | | | | |
| *The last column assumes a cycle time of 400 ns.* | | | | |
	name of benchmark	scavenge time (cycles)	data scavenged (words)	cycles per word	scavenge time (ms)
1	decompiler	56,832	2,477	23	23
2	decompiler	45,832	2,028	23	19
3	decompiler	45,491	2,022	22	18
4	decompiler	41,262	1,828	23	17
5	decompiler	69,937	3,114	22	27
6	decompiler	37,449	1,692	22	15
7	decompiler	37,157	1,693	23	16
8	decompiler	30,100	1,489	20	12
9	decompiler	29,228	1,489	20	12
10	printDefinition	63,417	2,542	25	25
11	printDefinition	53,535	2,587	21	22
12	compiler	60,374	2,834	21	24
	min	29,000	1,500	20	12
	25%ile	37,000	1,700	21	15
	median	45,000	2,000	22	18
	mean	48,000	2,200	22	19
	(s.d.)	(13,000)	(540)	(1.4)	(5.0)
	75%ile	57,000	2,500	23	23
	max	70,000	3,100	25	27

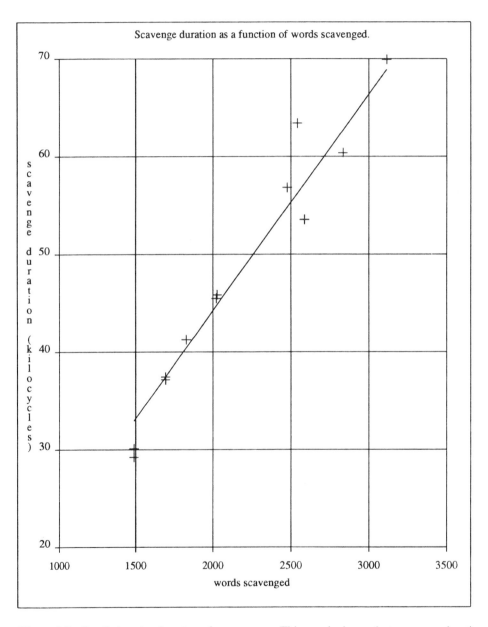

Figure 5.8: Predicting the duration of a scavenge. This graph shows that scavenge duration can be predicted from the number of words scavenged.

mean scavenge time was 19 ms, eight times less than BS's 160 ms. There are several possible explanations:

- A SOAR chip receives 32 bits from memory every cycle whereas the 68010 is limited to 16 bits. Thus the SOAR system has twice the memory bandwidth.

- The simulated SOAR scavenging copied less data than the BS scavenges. The most likely explanation is activation records; BS keeps them in new space forcing each scavenge to copy them. On the other hand, SOAR allocates activation records in a separate stack that gets scanned rather than copied. The numbers show that the average BS scavenge copied 4.8 Kwords whereas the average SOAR scavenge copied only 2.1 Kwords. This accounts for 2.3 times the work.

The above two explanations together account for a factor of 4.6, leaving a factor of 1.8 performance improvement to be explained by the next two differences (which are harder to quantify):

- Assembly code can be more efficient than C. Generation Scavenging is written in assembler for SOAR and in C for BS.

- SOAR's architecture runs programs faster than the 68010's. In particular, the reduced instruction set, register file, word addressing, fast shuffle, and tag checking hardware might contribute to the performance improvement of scavenging in SOAR.

5.9.2.2. SOAR Scavenge Frequency

The worst SOAR scavenge took 27 ms, which is well below the threshold for an annoying pause. However, if the time that a program could run between scavenge and the next were too short, the 27 ms pause would still be unacceptable. The length of this gap between pauses is determined by the creation rate for new objects and the by amount of memory available to hold them. To measure this interval, we ran six benchmarks on SOAR and measured the rate of object creation during a (randomly chosen) portion of each. The data are presented in Table 5.9. With 150 KB available for newly-created objects, 2.3 seconds of computation will be available to amortize the 27 ms scavenging pause. The creation rate would have to grow by an order of magnitude to be a problem.

5.9.2.3. Net SOAR Scavenge Overhead

Given the above data, we can calculate the pause time, gap between scavenges, and average scavenge overhead (Table 5.10). The results that generation scavenging is non-disruptive; a 27 ms pause every second is hard to notice. Furthermore, scavenging uses less than 2% of the CPU time, allowing the computation to proceed at full speed.

Table 5.9: Space allocation rate benchmarks on SOAR. *(Samples are complete second iterations of each benchmark.)* *(Assumes new area size = 150KB, cycle time = 400 ns.)*					
benchmark	duration (cycles)	space allocated (words)	growth rate (w/kc)	growth rate (kw/sec)	scavenge interval (secs)
decompiler	2,958,219	36,886	12	31	1.2
printHierarchy	119,040	1,426	12	30	1.3
allImplementors	2,257,051	18,058	8.0	20	1.9
printDefinition	75,319	509	6.8	17	2.3
compiler	1,117,660	7,467	6.7	17	2.3
classOrganizer	2,959,728	9,905	3.3	8.4	4.6
mean	—	—	8.1	21	2.3
s.d.	—	—	3.4	8.6	1.2

Table 5.10: Extrapolated vs. Simulated Scavenging on SOAR.			
	best case	average	worst case
pause time	12 ms	19 ms	27 ms
scavenge interval	4.6 secs	2.3 secs	1.2 secs
scavenge overhead	0.3%	0.8%	2.3%
trapping overhead	0%	0.05%	1.0%
total overhead	0.3%	0.9%	3.3%

5.9.2.4. Generation Scavenge Trap Time

Recall that the Generation Scavenging algorithm maintains a table of references from old to new objects. SOAR traps when it creates such a reference,
enabling the trap routine to enter the address of the referenced object in the table.
Table 5.11 gives an analysis of store trap overhead for the simulated macro
benchmarks. The path length of 100 cycles for a store trap was determined by
assuming a 1 in 8 chance of window overflow, and taking the worst case for the
other branches. The worst case overhead to maintain the remembered set is 1%,
with a median of 0.05%.

Table 5.11: Generation Scavenge Store trapping overhead in SOAR.				
Benchmark Name	Benchmark Cycles	store traps	store trap cycles	store trap overhead
decompiler	2,958,219	0	0	0%
allImplementors	2,257,051	1	100	0.004%
classOrganizer	2,959,728	14	1,400	0.05%
compiler	1,117,660	7	700	0.06%
printDefinition	75,319	1	100	0.13%
printHierarchy	119,040	12	1,200	1.0%
median				0.05%

5.9.3. Summary of Generation Scavenging's Performance

Table 5.12 summarizes our findings. See Appendix D for a more detailed description.

Generation Scavenging offers outstanding performance:

•   At 3%, its CPU overhead is three times lower than deferred reference counting, its nearest competitor on a compiled Smalltalk-80 system. The overhead is so low that designers of high-performance systems who formerly shunned automatic storage reclamation can now embrace it.

•   The short pause times for Generation Scavenging are a good match to an exploratory programming environment. Since people have difficulty noticing pauses of 100 ms, they will not be disturbed by pauses of 28 ms.

•   The 200 KB of main memory needed for temporary data exceeds the space requirements of most older algorithms. However, given the state of the art

Table 5.12: Summary of Generation Scavenging's Performance.		
	Berkeley Smalltalk	SOAR
execution model	interpreted	compiled
source of data	measurements	simulations
processor	MC68010	SOAR
cycle time	400 ns	400 ns
CPU time overhead		
mean	1.5%	0.9%
worst case	n.a.	3.3%
pause time (scavenge duration)		
mean	160 ms	19 ms
worst case	330 ms	28 ms
peak main memory usage	200 KB	200 KB
backing store accesses	0.15	n.a.

in computer memory hardware, 200 KB of overhead seems reasonable for a system with 2 MB of main memory.

- Ideally, automatic storage reclamation should not cause any page faults. Even without any provisions for locking new and *remembered* objects in main memory, BS averaged only 1 page fault per seven scavenges.

5.9.4. Performance Evaluation of Direct Addressing on SOAR

Because Generation Scavenging includes compaction, the usual indirection through an object table is unnecessary in BS and SOAR, making them the only Smalltalk-80 systems without object tables. The indirection through such a table is sometimes overlooked when evaluating reference-counting reclamation, but it can be a bottleneck; a typical Smalltalk-80 system accesses the object table 1.2 times per bytecode [UnP83]. Assuming SOAR performs as fast as the Dorado (300KB.c/.s), SOAR would access the object table 360,000 times per second. The absolute minimum table access would be a single load instruction. Assuming 400 ns per cycle, such an indirection would take two cycles, or 800 ns. At 360,000 table accesses per second, that would be 0.29 seconds of indirection time for each second of processing time. Discussions with Deutsch suggest that further optimization possibly could halve this overhead. In other words, an object table would slow SOAR by 15% to 29%.

Although we eliminated the object table to improve performance, there is one Smalltalk-80 primitive operation that runs much slower without it. The *become:* primitive exchanges the identities of two objects, so that all pointers to the first object are redirected to the second, and vice versa.

A Smalltalk-80 system with an object table can perform a *become* quickly by exchanging object table entries (Figure 5.9). A system without an object table (such as SOAR) must search objects and exchange pointers. Although we

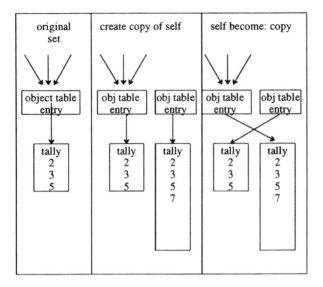

Figure 5.9: Growing with become. The sequence above illustrates how a Smalltalk-80 set employs become to grow. Initially, the set is {2, 3, 5} and we attempt to add 7 to it. The set creates a larger copy of itself and uses *become:* to replace the original set with the larger version.

have devised strategies to limit the search, a worst case *become* still involves a search throughout virtual memory. Such a long pause is unacceptable. We avoided this problem by rewriting the software for Smalltalk-80 data structures to avoid *becomes*. To establish the feasibility of this approach, we added new Collection classes that mimic old ones without resorting to *becomes* (Figure 5.10), then modified the macro-benchmarks to take advantage of our *become*-less classes [Wal83]. Table 5.13 presents an analysis of this change on system performance. The printDefinition benchmark shows that this change has a negligible effect on a benchmark that does not do any *becomes*. But, our efforts to eliminate *becomes* from programs that did use them were handsomely repaid with an 18% to 28% performance improvement.

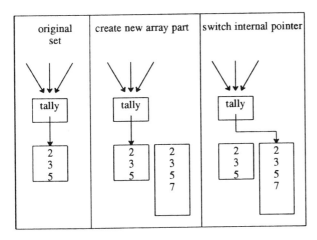

Figure 5.10: Growing without become. The sequence above illustrates how our modified sets grow without resorting to *become:*. The contents are stored in a separate array. To grow, the set allocates a larger array, initializes it, and redirects an internal point to the new array. We have replaced costly implicit indirection with explicit indirection that incurs cost only when needed. This is in keeping with the RISC philosophy.

Table 5.13: Performance impact of eliminating becomes.				
benchmark	# becomes	duration w/ becomes (cycles)	duration w/o becomes (cycles)	cycles saved
printDefinition	0	75,475	75,317	0%
compiler	7	1,383,201	1,127,658	18%
decompiler	38	4,045,641	3,006,974	26%
printHierarchy	3	165,997	119,574	28%

Although we have eliminated *becomes* invoked by the system classes, the SOAR programmer must either shy away from this primitive, or be prepared to pay a stiff performance penalty. Forcing the user to worry about the efficiency a primitive operation runs counter to the philosophy of exploratory programming environments in general and Smalltalk-80 in particular. However, we believe that the *become* primitive is so intrinsically expensive—fast *becomes* require a level of indirection that slows down many frequent operations—that the effort to accomplish a *become* should not be hidden.

We have also estimated the impact of indirection on code size. An Object Table would require an extra instruction to load or store a literal variable, and one indirection in the method prologue (for the receiver). (We are assuming that many indirections will be optimized away, as in Deutsch and Schiffman's system.) Table 5.14 presents our analysis under these assumptions. The extra code for an object table would add only 2% to the size of the system.

5.9.5. Architectural support for Storage Management

The SOAR chip supports demand-paged virtual memory with restartable, fixed sized instructions and a page fault interrupt [SKF85]. An off-chip page map translates addresses and maintains referenced information. The silicon cost for virtual memory is about 20 support chips including the page map. Figure 5.11 shows that the SOAR host board hides the page map access time in memory access time [BlD83].

To support Generation Scavenging, all pointers include a four-bit tag. When a store instruction stores a new pointer into an old object, a special trap occurs. The software trap handler then records the reference. The tag-checking PLA has 8 inputs and one output, and occupies about 0.1% of the total chip area.

Table 5.14: Static cost of object indirection.	
method prologues	4654
literal variable loads	3532
literal variable stores	254
total image size	1,500 kB
relative cost of additional code	2.25%

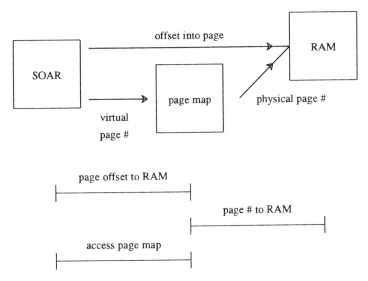

Figure 5.11: Fast address translation. The SOAR system has adopted the same technique as the Sun 68010 workstation to perform address translation without hurting performance. It hides the translation time in the address multiplexing delay for the dynamic RAM chips. On each memory access, the low order address bits that specify the offset into the page are sent to the memory while simultaneously reading the page map. The physical page number is then sent to the memory as the second piece of the address. A virtual memory with one segment per object could not run as fast because the offset into a segment is not identical to the least significant bits of the physical address. Consequently, no portion of the virtual address can be sent immediately to the RAM chips.

The cost of the extra control logic to handle the trap is harder to measure. As mentioned in Chapter 4, tagged store instructions occur so rarely that even this small cost cannot be justified.

5.9.6. Generation Scavenging and Activation Records

We have simplified this chapter by deliberately omitting activation records. In this section, we outline the problems caused by activation records in Smalltalk-80 and our solutions to them. Activation records present a problem because a Smalltalk-80 program can manipulate them like any other object. For instance, a subroutine can obtain a pointer to its activation record and place it in a global variable. After the subroutine returns, another routine can inspect the activation record via the global variable. Since SOAR activation records are kept in the register frame stack, extraordinary measures are required to preserve this information. When a Smalltalk-80 program creates a reference to an activation record we mark it as *non-lifo*. When a *non-lifo* activation is about to be destroyed (i.e. when a return instruction attempts to free it), we copy the record to the heap and adjust the references to it. Thus, the steps are:

1) *Detect the creation of a non-lifo reference to an activation record, then mark the activation record as non-lifo:*

    A non-lifo reference can be created by storing a pointer to an activation record or by returning such a pointer as a result. We have allocated a distinct tag for activation records (context, or 1111). A tagged store instruction will trap when storing such a pointer. As for returns, the SOAR compiler generates a trap instruction before each return that checks the tag and traps if needed. The trap handler sets the high-order bit of the activation record's return address. This marks the activation record as non-lifo. Meanwhile, the reference is added to a software table so it can be updated later.

2) *Detect a return from a non-lifo activation record, then copy it and update any references to it.*

    The return instruction traps if the return address has its high-order bit set. This trap handler then allocates space in the new area for the activation record, copies it, and updates references to it. At this point there is no need to trap further stores, so the reference's tag is changed to new.

We have extended this strategy to include blocks. Smalltalk-80 blocks implement control structures by allowing one routine to control execution in another's context. Frequently, a block is created, passed down the call chain to a subroutine that repeatedly invokes the block and then returns. Thus, we must impose a minimum of overhead on this case, while handling non-lifo references to blocks. In other words, although a block is an object that refers to a context, we do not mark the context as non-lifo until the block itself becomes non-lifo. This is accomplished with the same mechanism outlined above; using the context tag for block objects.

5.9.7. The Potential Problem of Premature Promotion

Recall that Generation Scavenging is based on the assumption that the longer an object survives the longer it will remain alive. Therefore, when an object attains a ripe old age, it is promoted from the new generation to the old. At this point, the system assumes that the object is immortal and ceases attempts to reclaim it. For this reason, we call the promotion process *tenuring*. However, in some cases the object may die shortly thereafter and waste space long after its useful life.

At first glance, one would expect dead tenured objects to waste backing storage, but not main memory. They would seem to get paged out to make room for tenured objects that remain alive. However, because an object is so small relative to the size of a page (14 vs. 1024 words), a page could easily contain just a few live objects among many dead ones. This internal fragmentation could tie up much more main memory than is actually needed for the live objects. In this manner dead tenured objects can increase the number of pages in the working set.

How severe is this problem? We plan to reclaim dead tenured objects once a day by an offline reclamation program. How many will build up in a day? We won't know until we measure the lifetimes of objects over hours of elapsed time on a high-performance system like the Dorado or SOAR. Chapter 6 has a more detailed discussion of this issue and strategies for coping, should it turn out to be a problem.

5.10. Summary of Reclamation Algorithms

Table 5.15 summarizes our results: both Deutsch-Bobrow deferred reference counting and Generation Scavenging perform well enough for an advanced personal computer. The advantages of Generation Scavenging over deferred reference counting are:

- it reclaims circular structures,

- it includes compaction, and

- it uses less than a tenth of the total CPU time.

Table 5.15: Summary of reclamation strategies.					
	CPU time	main memory for dynamic objects	paging I/Os	pause time (sec)	pause interval (sec)
page it, no reclamation	?	15 KB	~50/s		
immed ref. count (compaction)	15% - 20%	15 KB	?	0 1.3	∞ 60 - 1200
deferred ref. count (compaction)	11%	40 KB	?	0.030 1.3	0.30 60 - 1200
mark and sweep	25% - 40%	1900 KB	90/gc	4.5	74
Ballard	7%*	2000 KB	0	0	∞
Generation Scavenging					
BS	2%	200 KB	1.2/s	0.16	16
SOAR best case	0.3%	170KB	0	0.011	4.0
SOAR average	0.9%	170KB	0	0.017	2.0
SOAR worst case	3.3%	170KB	0	0.025	1.1

* Ballard's Smalltalk-80 system used interpretive execution. Although using a VAX 11/780 it ran the compiler macro-benchmark five times slower than Deutsch's deferred reference counting dynamically compiled Xerox ST68K system [BaS83, DeS84]. Ballard's storage reclamation algorithm may well exceed 7% overhead on a compiled Smalltalk-80 system.

5.11. Conclusions

The combination of generation scavenging and paging provides high performance automatic storage reclamation, compaction, and virtual memory. This method of storage management has proven its worth daily in Berkeley Smalltalk, which has supported the SOAR compiler project, architectural studies, and text editing for portions of this chapter.

The algorithm we have presented may not accommodate objects that live for a medium amount of time; they may increase the time overhead or cause thrashing. Measurements must be taken on high-performance Smalltalk-80 systems to understand the behavior of these objects.

High performance storage reclamation relies on two principles:

- Young objects die young. Therefore a reclamation algorithm should not waste time on old objects.

- For young objects, fatalities overwhelm survivors. Copying survivors is much cheaper than scanning corpses.

Careful consideration of the virtual memory system is essential. Generation Scavenging combines these lessons to meet stringent performance goals: low time overhead (2% in BS, 3% in SOAR), imperceptibly short pause times (160 ms in BS, 27 ms in SOAR), and a low page fault rate (1.2 faults/sec in BS). Meeting these goals costs 200 KB of primary memory, but the result is worth it; a high-performance computer system with fast automatic storage reclamation.

Chapter 6

Scavenging Data with Intermediate Lifetimes

6.1. Introduction

What happens if the age of an object fails to predict its lifetime? An object that survives long enough to be promoted but succumbs shortly thereafter will waste storage in old space. This chapter contains a detailed description of the problem, how we have attacked in Berkeley Smalltalk, some proposals for extra generations, and an analytical model that sheds some light on the effect of various parameters on performance.

6.2. The Tenuring Threshold

When should Generation Scavenging tenure an object? Since we have observed that young objects are likely to die and old ones are likely to persist, our algorithm tenures an object that lives long enough. The easiest way to measure age is to count the number of scavenges an object survives. Thus, each object contains a byte that is initialized to zero and is incremented on each scavenge. If an object survives for a certain number of scavenges, it gets tenured. The problem is to choose this threshold. If it is too small, that is if Generation Scavenging tenures objects too soon, a large fraction of them will die shortly after receiving tenure. Tenured garbage wastes space on backing store, and more importantly, may slow the system with extra page faults by mixing dead and live objects on the same page. On the other hand, if the tenuring threshold is too high, long-lived objects will pile up in the new area, increasing the amount of data that must be copied for each scavenge. This will increase the pause time and the CPU overhead for storage reclamation. Thus, the tenuring threshold must balance the increase in page faults caused by tenured garbage against the extra pause time caused by scavenging long-lived objects.

In Berkeley Smalltalk, we have included a feedback-mediated adaptive algorithm to set the tenuring threshold. The algorithm examines the amount of data that survived the previous scavenge and adjusts the tenuring threshold accordingly. The current implementation limits the tenuring threshold to 64, where it remains most of the time. On SOAR, a tenuring threshold of 64 would mean that an object would have to survive for more than a minute to be tenured. Since the response time for most requests is much smaller than a minute, setting the tenuring threshold to 64 would allow Generation Scavenging to reclaim the bulk of the garbage online.

We have performed an experiment with BS to better understand tenuring. Since the objects of concern are those that live for relatively long times, a typical interactive session of several hours duration would be ideal for characterizing tenuring behavior. Berkeley Smalltalk's poor overall performance, 10% of a Dorado, prevented us from gathering data from a typical interactive session. Lacking a Dorado or SOAR chip, we settled for a synthetic workload: our image merely ran the decompiler benchmark twenty times. The interval between scavenges was held fairly constant while varying the tenure threshold. A total of 20kw was allocated in the new area (plus 20kw for each survivor area). The feedback mediated scavenge algorithm used an average of 18.7 kw before each scavenge. Table 6.1 gives our results.

Figure 6.1 shows the relationship between the tenuring threshold and the number of bytes of data that were tenured. As expected, the number of objects achieving tenure decreases as the time required to obtain tenure increases. In addition, there are two knees in the curve — also just as expected. The first knee, at a tenure threshold of one, merely proves that most objects die very quickly.

Table 6.1: Results of BS tenuring experiment.						
tenure threshold (# gs's)	# gs's	total time (secs)	total tenured (kw)	avg. surv. (kw)	max surv. (kw)	CPU time overhead (%)*
0	90	340	56.0	2.3	4.3	0.6%
1	83	290	17.0	2.9	4.3	0.8%
2	83	310	16.9	3.0	4.3	0.8%
3	83	300	16.7	3.2	4.5	0.9%
4	83	290	3.7	3.4	4.8	0.9%
5	83	300	3.7	3.4	4.6	0.9%
6	83	300	3.9	3.5	4.6	0.9%
7	83	280	3.7	3.5	4.7	1.0%
8	83	290	3.6	3.6	4.8	1.0%
16	83	290	2.9	3.8	4.9	1.0%
32	83	300	2.4	4.2	6.9	1.1%
64	83	290	2.0	5.1	6.4	1.4%

The reason is that a threshold of zero means that every object gets promoted—even though it may be only milliseconds old—but a threshold of one means that an object that gets promoted must be older than the time between scavenges. Since the scavenges occurred every 3.5 seconds, this knee shows that many objects live less than 3.5 seconds.

The second knee, at 4, indicates that many objects live for more than 3×3.5 seconds but less than 4×3.5 seconds. This is not surprising because each iteration of the benchmark took about 12 seconds. The only objects tenured at a threshold of 4, were those that survived for more than one iteration. These were the text lines printed on the screen from the benchmarks. This experiment confirms our understanding of tenuring; any object which outlives the product of the tenuring threshold and the inter-scavenge time gets tenured.

---

* Based on 24 cycles * survivor + 3500 as derived in Section 5.9.2.1.

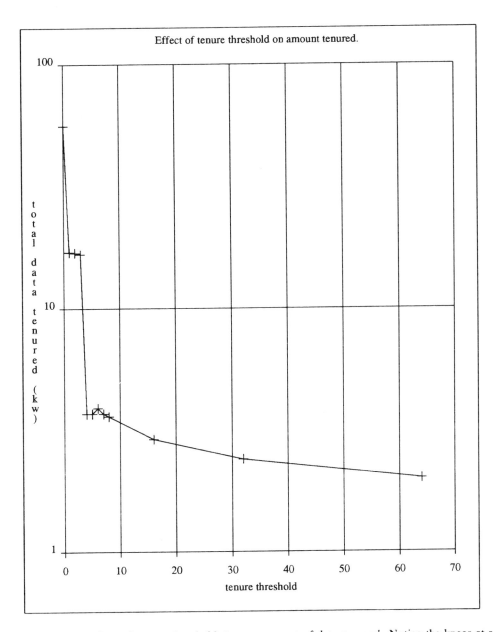

Figure 6.1: Effect of tenure threshold time on amount of data tenured. Notice the knees at a tenure threshold of 1 and 4.

Although minimizing the amount of tenured data saves (virtual) memory space and improves paging performance, it forces the scavenge operation to copy more survivors, which takes more time. The surprise is how small this increase is. In this experiment, the quantity of tenured data—which is principally garbage—decreased by a factor of 23, while the time spent on scavenging merely doubled.

Unfortunately, we would need measurements of a fast Smalltalk-80 system to completely predict the effects of tenuring. Tenuring affects objects that live for minutes or hours. These objects are used by people, not programs. For example, the objects that comprise a window on a screen would have lifetimes of minutes. Because their lifetimes depend on how people use them, we cannot extrapolate from a slow Smalltalk-80 system such as BS to a fast one like SOAR.

Although we cannot characterize the problem, we can characterize some potential solutions:

1. *Two generations with fast tenuring.* This is the present configuration. Deutsch has estimated that data structures used by a typical window, for example a browser, consume 15 KB of memory. At 20 cycles per word, that means that it would take 30 ms to scavenge the data for a window. Thus, assuming 150 KB of new space, every untenured window would add 3% to the scavenging overhead, limiting the number of untenured windows to about 4. If the rate of window creation is slow enough, a system that tenures objects so fast that every window gets tenured may be practical. On the other hand, if many windows are created and immediately destroyed (as in the case of error message windows) it may be important to retain a few untenured windows.

2. *Two generations with slow tenuring.* Assume we dedicate a megabyte of physical memory to new objects. Then the system can run seven seconds

between scavenges. That means that a more data can be scavenged without incurring incurring excessive overhead. In fact, the limit becomes the scavenge's pause time, not the percentage of overhead. Suppose that we accept a fifth-second pause every seven seconds. That is long enough to scavenge seven windows. This may be a sufficient number of untenured windows to avoid tenuring garbage. (Interestingly, seven is roughly the size of a human short-term memory.)

3. *Three generations with fast tenuring.* Suppose we add a third generation in the middle. Some of the space for the third generation can be obtained by reducing the size of the youngest generation from 100KB to 50KB, which triples the scavenge overhead to a (still acceptable) 3%. A middle generation of 300KB of physical memory can contain ten untenured windows (in each semispace). The time for a scavenge of the middle generation would be about 300 ms. This option can support about the same number of windows as the two generation, slow tenuring one, but with slightly more space and significantly less time overhead.

4. *Three generations with slow tenuring.* Suppose we add a large third generation, but use virtual memory instead of physical. Scavenging this middle-aged generation would then incur page faults and cause a perceptible pause, perhaps one to three seconds. However, 30 windows could be created before filling (the 1/2 MB semispace of) a one megabyte generation. Thus, these long scavenges would be infrequent, and acceptable.

5. *Four generations.* SOAR's tags support four generations, so we could combine the above schemes. The youngest generation would be small, locked into memory, and frequently scavenged. An object surviving two scavenges would be promoted into the next generation. This would also be in physical memory, but larger. This generation would hold the newest few

windows. Thus, this is important if many windows are closed immediately. The third generation, would be about a megabyte, and located in virtual memory. Most windows and medium lifetime objects would reside here. They could be reclaimed without a complete reorganization. Finally, permanent objects like the square-root routine would reside in the oldest generation, which would be reclaimed and reorganized offline. Table 6.2 summarized these proposals. More work is needed to measure the behavior of these medium lifetime objects and to design appropriate two- or three- generation parameters and reorganization algorithms.

6.3. Analysis of a Single Scavenged Generation

How much physical memory must be dedicated to new objects? In this section we present an analysis of a two-generation system where one generation is scavenged (New) and the other is reclaimed offline (Old). Since the Old objects are reclaimed offline, we will only analyze the New generation here. Table 6.3 introduces the relevant terms. The first constraint we face is to keep the scavenge pauses small enough to be unobtrusive. The data on scavenging duration in the previous section showed that the length of a scavenge can be predicted from the amount of data surviving the scavenge.

$$pause = (se \times ct) \times surv \tag{1}$$

Let's test this with an example. Plugging in typical SOAR parameters $ct = 400ns$, $se = 5.5cyc/byte$, and $surv = 8,800bytes$:

$$pause = (5.5 \times 400ns) \times 8,800 = 19ms \tag{1E}$$

which matches the simulated pause time of 19 ms.

Reducing the tenuring threshold will limit the quantity of data that survives a scavenge by promoting the oldest surviving objects. Once in Old space, they

Table 6.2:	Summary of tenuring proposals.				
generation		assistant	associate	full	emeritus
type of memory		physical		virtual	
Proposal 1. Two generations, fast tenuring.					
creation area	(KB)	140			4,000
gap time	(sec)	1			?
survivor area	(KB)	17			disk
pause time	(ms)	30			60
scavenge time	(%)	3%			?
primary memory	(KB)	170			2,000
Proposal 2. Two generations, slow tenuring.					
creation area	(KB)	420			4,000
gap time	(sec)	3			?
survivor area	(KB)	170			disk
pause time	(sec)	0.30			60
scavenge time	(%)	10%			?
primary memory	(KB)	760			2,000
Proposal 3. Three generations, fast tenuring.					
creation area	(KB)	140	0		4,000
gap time	(sec)	1	600		?
survivor area	(KB)	17	150		disk
pause time	(sec)	0.030	0.30		60
scavenge time	(%)	3%	0.05%		?
primary memory (KB)		170	300		1 – 3 MB
Proposal 4. Three generations, slow tenuring.					
creation area	(KB)	140		0	3,000
gap time	(sec)	1		2,000	?
survivor area	(KB)	17		500	disk
pause time	(sec)	0.030		$^-10$	60
scavenge time	(%)	3%		0.5%	?
primary memory (KB)		170		500	0.5 – 2.5 MB
Proposal 5. Four generations.					
creation area	(KB)	140	0	0	3,000
gap time	(sec)	1	600	20,000?	?
survivor area	(KB)	17	150	500	disk
pause time	(sec)	0.030	0.30	$^-10$	60
scavenge time	(%)	3%	0.05%	0.05%?	?
primary memory (KB)		170	300	500	0.5 – 2.5 MB

Table 6.3: Quantities to analyze a single generation.		
symbol	*description*	*units*
constants		
ct	SOAR cycle time	seconds
se	scavenge effort: avg. cycles per scavenged byte	cycles per byte
abw	allocation bandwidth: rate of new data instantiation	bytes per second
independent variables		
surv	size of each survivor area	bytes
Eden	size of new object creation area	bytes
dependent variables		
mem	total memory used	bytes
pause	length of scavenging pause	seconds
gap	gap between scavenges	seconds
ov	fraction of CPU used for scavenging this generation	fraction [0, 1]

need not be scavenged. But, as discussed in the previous section, too much tenuring can provoke thrashing. Thus, we recommend choosing an acceptable pause time (perhaps from 10 ms to 100 ms) and adaptively adjusting the tenure threshold to maintain the corresponding amount of untenured data.

The next step is to calculate the amount of memory devoted to newly-created objects. Let's assume that the rate of object allocation is fairly constant. Then

$$gap = \frac{Eden}{abw} \tag{2}$$

For example, in the growth rate experiment in the previous section, we found that the compiler benchmark generated 17,000 words per second. Thus, $abw = 68,000 bytes/sec$, so for $Eden = 150,000$,

$$gap = \frac{150,000}{68,000} = 2.2 sec \tag{2E}$$

In other words, with 150 KB for new objects, SOAR could run for two seconds between successive scavenges.

Although, $ov = \dfrac{pause}{pause + gap}$, we will use a simpler approximation,

$$ov = \frac{pause}{gap} \tag{3}$$

for our analysis. (This is a reasonable approximation because we only care about systems with low overhead.) Continuing with our example, we can use equation (3) to calculate the time overhead:

$$ov = \frac{19ms}{2.2sec} = 0.86\% \tag{3E}$$

Since we have expressions for the pause and gap times, we can combine (1), (2), and (3) to express the overhead in terms of memory allocations:

$$\frac{surv}{Eden} = \frac{ov}{(se \times ct \times abw)} \tag{4}$$

Suppose we need to decide how much memory to allocate for Eden in SOAR:

$$\frac{8600}{Eden} = \frac{ov}{0.15}$$

$$Eden \times ov = 1300KB \tag{4E}$$

So, for 2% overhead, we would allocate 65 KB to Eden. This would total $2 \times 8600 + 65,000 = 82KB$ of main memory for New objects.

For the general case we can combine

$$mem = Eden + 2 \times surv \tag{5}$$

with (4) to calculate the total memory required. Suppose we built the system as described above, only to discover that it tenures too much garbage. The first step to cut down on tenuring would be to boost the quantity of untenured survivors. This will increase the pause time for a scavenge; equation (1) says that $surv = \frac{pause}{2 \times 10^{-6}}$. Thus, 50 KB of survivors will result in pauses that last 100 ms. The increased pause time will drive up CPU overhead unless we dedicate more memory to Eden. Suppose we allow CPU overhead to rise to 5% to economize on memory, then equation (4) gives the size of the Eden area required.

$$\frac{50{,}000}{Eden} = \frac{0.05}{0.15} = 0.33$$

$$Eden = \frac{50{,}000}{0.33} = 150{,}000$$

Equation (5) then supplies the total memory for this generation:

$$memory = 150{,}000 + 2 \times 50{,}000 = 250{,}000 \tag{5E}$$

6.4. Analyzing a Middle Generation

What if this is still not enough space for medium-lifetime objects? A third generation can be added in the middle. This results in a system with three generations: a generation for evanescent objects (Generation 1), a generation for medium-lived objects (Generation 2), and a generation for permanent objects (Figure 6.2). Assuming that we keep Generation 2 in primary memory, how are we going to divide memory among the two scavenged generations? The equations in the previous section specify the behavior of a single scavenged generation, so we can apply them to each of the two scavenged generations, using subscripts to indicate the generation. Then, by superposition from (4):

$$ov = ov_1 + ov_2 = \frac{(se_1 \times ct_1 \times abw_1)surv_1}{Eden_1} + \frac{(se_2 \times ct_2 \times abw_2)surv_2}{Eden_2} \tag{6}$$

For example, assume that each window uses 15 KB of data, and that we want to be able to support ten windows without tenuring. Then $surv_2 = 150KB$. If we open one window per minute, $abw_2 = 15\frac{KB}{60} = 250bytes/sec$. (Se and ct are the same for both generations.) Thus,

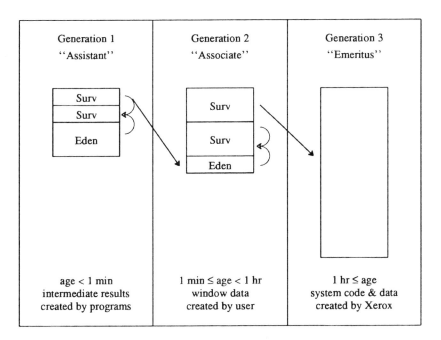

Figure 6.2: Diagram of a system with a middle generation. Objects are created in the Eden area of the Assistant generation. If an objects lives through several scavenges in the Assistant survivor areas, it gets promoted into the Associate Eden area. If it then survives scavenges between the Associate survivor areas, the object receives tenure into the Emeritus area, where it is exempt from online reclamation. Ideally, the parameters would be set to keep short-lived objects representing intermediate results in Generation 1, medium-lifetime objects used by windows in Generation 2, and long-lived objects like the square root routine in the Old generation.

$$ov = ov_1 + ov_2 = \frac{1300}{Eden_1} + \frac{74}{Eden_2} \tag{6E}$$

Now, let's minimize the total time overhead given a fixed amount of memory to divide among the two Edens. From (6), substituting $Eden_2 = Eden - Eden_1$ and differentiating with respect to $Eden_1$:

$$\frac{d\,(ov)}{(d\,Eden_1)} = -\frac{(se_1 \times ct_1 \times abw_1)surv_1}{Eden_1^2} + \frac{(se_2 \times ct_2 \times abw_2)surv_2}{(Eden - Eden_1)^2} \tag{7}$$

Setting $\dfrac{d\,(ov)}{(d\,Eden_1)} = 0$, and solving for $Eden_1$, we get

$$\frac{Eden_1}{Eden} = \cfrac{1}{1+\cfrac{\sqrt{(se_2{\times}ct_2{\times}abw_2)surv_2}}{\sqrt{(se_1{\times}ct_1{\times}abw_1)surv_1}}} \quad \text{and}$$

$$\frac{Eden_2}{Eden} = \cfrac{1}{1+\cfrac{\sqrt{(se_1{\times}ct_1{\times}abw_1)surv_1}}{\sqrt{(se_2{\times}ct_2{\times}abw_2)surv_2}}} \tag{8}$$

Continuing with our example,

$$\frac{Eden_1}{Eden} = \cfrac{1}{1+\cfrac{\sqrt{74}}{\sqrt{1300}}} = 81\% \quad\text{and}\quad \frac{Eden_2}{Eden} = \cfrac{1}{1+\cfrac{\sqrt{1300}}{\sqrt{74}}} = 19\% \tag{8E}$$

Given an optimal split, we can plug (8) into (5) to find the minimum amount of overhead for a given amount of memory:

$$ov{\times}Eden = \left[\sqrt{(se_1{\times}ct_1{\times}abw_1)surv_1}+\sqrt{(se_2{\times}ct_2{\times}abw_2)surv_2}\right]^2 \tag{9}$$

For our example,

$$ov{\times}Eden = \left[\sqrt{1300}+\sqrt{74}\right]^2 = 2000 \tag{9E}$$

So, for 2% overhead, 100 KB of Eden would be needed. Adding in the survivor areas, 420 KB of physical memory would be used for scavenging. What about those long pauses for Generation 2? From (1), $pause_2 = 150{,}000{\times}se{\times}ct = 300ms$.

From (5), $gap_2 = \dfrac{Eden_2}{abw_2} = \dfrac{0.19{\times}100KB}{250} = 76\,secs$. Thus, by adding a middle generation, we have made it possible to scavenge more untenured data by increasing the gap between long scavenges. This lets us keep 160 KB of untenured data in 420 KB of main memory at a time cost of 2.0%.

We may decide that minimizing the total CPU overhead is not as important as reducing the frequency of long pauses. In that case, we can abandon (8) and use (1) and (2). Suppose we can only tolerate a 300 ms pause once every 3 minutes. Then, using (2) $Eden_2 = 180{\times}250 = 45KB$. Assuming we use the same amount of memory as above, that leaves 55 KB for $Eden_1$. This results in a 0.81 second gap for Generation 1. With these parameters the total overhead is $\dfrac{19}{810} + \dfrac{300}{180,000} = 2.5\%$. Of course, this is worse than the optimal overhead of 2.0%.

6.5. Controlling the Tenuring Threshold

Objects must be tenured to avoid excessive pauses caused by scavenging too much data. The problem is to set the tenure threshold given the survivors from the past generation. We propose that a scavenge also maintain a table giving the total amount of surviving data for each age. Such a table could then be used to predict the amount of data that would be promoted for any given tenure threshold. Building this table would add about 10% to the scavenge time.

6.6. The Cost of an Offline Reorganization

To better understand the time required by an offline reorganization, we measured one on BS, on a diskless Sun 68010 workstation. Table 6.4 gives the results: this reorganization software is slow; 1200 memory cycles are expended in user mode on each word. Address space limitations of early Suns forced us to reorganize the old objects by copying them to a file, and modifying them in the file. Thus, every time a word is read from old space, a file read subroutine is called. Current Suns and SOAR have 16 MB of address space, more than

Table 6.4: Measurements of an offline reorganization on BS.	
user time	116.7
system time	46.1 sec
real time	179 sec
idle time	16 sec
CPU utilization	90.9%
reads	464
writes	492
page faults	14
initial old size	245,036 words
final old size	231,207 words
bandwidth	480 µs/word
16-bit cycles/word	1200

enough to hold a copy of the 1 MB to 2 MB of old space. Replacing file read/write software with virtual memory hardware should result in a large speed up, and a sub-minute reorganization seems feasible.

6.7. Summary

Objects that live long enough to be promoted but die shortly thereafter can present a problem for Generation Scavenging. To study this phenomonon, we would need data from sessions on high-performance systems using Generation Scavenging. Since we do not have the capability to perform these experiments, we have merely explored some solutions that can be adopted if necessary. The simplest strategy would be to tenuring threshold at a good compromise between time and space efficiency. If that did not suffice it might be necessary to add one or two more generations.

Chapter 7

Conclusions

7.1. Conclusions

We have presented and evaluated the hardware and software design of Smalltalk On A RISC (SOAR). We undertook this effort to see how well the reduced instruction set computer style of system design would work for a software environment heretofore supported only by complicated virtual machines. It has worked very well indeed. A combination of hardware and software strategies has allowed us to build a single-chip NMOS microprocessor that will match the performance of an ECL minicomputer, despite a 5:1 cycle time handicap. With about half of the transistors of the MC68010 microprocessor, a 400 ns SOAR will run the Smalltalk-80 system 2.5 times faster than the 400 ns MC68010. With only one fifth of the transistors of the MC68020, and with a handicap of about a factor of two in cycle time, SOAR will outrun the MC68020. RISCs pay off for experimental programming environments.

SOAR's performance comes at a price; namely, memory space. A bytecoded 32-bit Smalltalk-80 image occupies a megabyte of memory. Generation Scavenging adds 200 Kb to this, and compiling to a simple instruction set costs another 500 Kb. With current hardware technology, the extra 700 Kb is a small price to pay for high speed.

The most important hardware features are register windows and tagged integer instructions. These two features nearly double SOAR's performance by reducing the cost of subroutine calls and type-checked integer operations. Other important hardware features include byte insert/extract instructions, two-tone instructions, forwarding, one cycle jumps and calls, and tagged immediate data. In the realm of software, our storage management strategies (discussed below), direct pointers, in-line caching, and compiling to a simple instruction set are essential. In addition to permitting fast instruction decoding, the simplicity of the base architecture enables us to add the language-specific extensions.

On the other hand, despite our best intentions, we included several superfluous features in SOAR, including hardware support for storage reclamation, pointers to registers, parallel nilling, and shadow registers to aid trap handling. These are *architect's traps* because they increase design time and potentially increase the cycle time without appreciable reducing the number of cycles. These traps are baited with speedups for specific operations, and sprung when real programs fail to perform the optimized operations.

We believe that the key to good performance is a willingness to migrate functionality from one level of abstraction to another, viewing the system as a whole rather than as a collection of layers. During the design process, we moved functions freely up and down the implementation hierarchy from software to silicon to achieve good performance with minimal hardware. For example, instead of interpretation, we have chosen to burden the software with compiling and debugging a simple instruction set that can be executed quickly. Also, we have replaced microcoded instructions for infrequent operations with software trap handlers. Our system was designed with an implementation technology in mind; this is the opposite of separating the architecture from the hardware implementation.

We have developed an algorithm for automatic storage reclamation, Generation Scavenging, that permits SOAR to be the first full-speed Smalltalk-80 system without an object table. We have shown that, unlike many competing algorithms, Generation Scavenging requires no hardware support. In addition, this algorithm reduces the time spent on storage reclamation to 3% of the CPU time.

This is three times better than other Smalltalk-80 systems with comparable performance. Finally, unlike traditional reference-counting algorithms, Generation Scavenging can reclaim circular structures of dead objects. Automatic storage reclamation is no longer an important source of overhead.

SOAR represents a substantial improvement in cost-performance over previous Smalltalk-80 systems. We recommend that anyone faced with the task of building a computer for an exploratory programming environment consider compilation to a reduced instruction set.

7.2. Future Work

At this date SOAR has been fabricated and, running at 800 ns., has successfully completed all of its diagnostics [Pen85b]. An unforeseen critical path to memory needed by the fast shuffle hardware has increased its cycle time from 400 ns to 510 ns. Samples has ported the Smalltalk-80 system to the SOAR simulator; the system starts up and displays its windows on the screen. Our goal is to run the Smalltalk-80 system on SOAR. We will then measure the performance of the system to find any flaws lurking in our performance data. One of the most interesting remaining tasks is to construct a debugger for SOAR that provides all the functionality of the current Smalltalk-80 bytecode debugger. A Smalltalk-80 system running on SOAR with complete, source-level debugging facilities would demonstrate that the primitive level of the instruction set can be hidden from the user. Finally, Pendleton has proposed reimplementing a stripped-down SOAR with an optimized pipeline in a more advanced VLSI technology to yield a very fast Smalltalk-80 system.

One aspect of Generation Scavenging remains in dire need of exploration: objects with an intermediate life span. If promoted too soon, they waste disk space and can degrade virtual memory performance. If promoted too late, they waste the CPU time needed to repeatedly scavenge them. Adding a third, middle generation is a possibility. Further research will require measurements of high-performance Smalltalk-80 systems with real users to obtain realistic actuarial data.

7.3. Acknowledgments

Many have contributed to SOAR's success:

Many students at Berkeley contributed to studies that helped determine SOAR's architecture: Scott Baden, John Blakken, Wayne Citrin, Tom Conroy, Bruce D'Ambrosio, Robert Hagmann, Edward Pelegri-Llopart, Carl Ponder, Richard Probst, Harry Rubin, Stuart Sechrest, Tim Sippel, and Paul Strauss.

We were fortunate to have first-rate CAD tools on hand built by Gordon Hamachi, Bob Mayo, George Taylor, Walter Scott, Ken Keller, Deirdre Ryan, Richard Rudell, John Foderaro, and Jim Larus, on teams led by John Ousterhout, Richard Newton, and Alberto Sangiovanni-Vincentelli. Pete Foley originally designed our datapath and control, which Joan Pendleton later redesigned and built.

David Hodges led the hardware efforts. Joan Pendleton is responsible for NMOS implementation, assisted by Shin Kong with contributions by Artie Chang, Mike Klein, and Mike Remillard. The CMOS chip, completed by Chris Marino, started as a group effort with B. K. Bose, Mark Hofmann, Grace Mah, H. Mattausch, Peter Moore, B. Schallenberger, Dave Wallace, and John Zapisek. Our two circuit boards were designed and tested by Will Brown, Frank Dunlap, Richard Blomseth and Helen Davis on workstations donated by the Valid Logic corporation.

Paul Hilfinger led the software effort and built our first compiler, while Dain Samples, Ricki Blau and Bill Bush provided our simulator and system software, assembler and diagnostics, and compiler. Dain also gets special thanks for writing our internal reference manuals.

Adele Goldberg, Ted Kaehler, Glenn Krasner, and Dan Ingalls of the Systems Concepts Group at Xerox PARC gave us a lot of assistance in understanding Smalltalk. Peter Deutsch, of that group, deserves special recognition for serving as our liaison with Xerox, and spending a lot of time and effort helping us understand Smalltalk systems. He and Alan Schiffman of Fairchild have built the fastest Smalltalk-80 system on a commercial microprocessor, and we learned a lot from them.

We also thank MOSIS and Xerox, including Ed McCreight, J. Chen, and B. Pugh for fabricating SOAR, and Paul Losleben and V. Tyree at DARPA for funding the project. This project was sponsored by Defense Advance Research Projects Agency (DoD) ARPA Order No. 3803, monitored by Naval Electronic System Command under Contract No. N00034-K-0251. It was also sponsored by Defense Advance Research Projects Agency (DoD) ARPA Order No. 4871, monitored by Naval Electronic Systems Command under Contract No. N00039-84-C-0089. The University of California, the state of California, and IBM provided me with indispensable financial support.

Please join me in acknowledging the efforts of the people who read through this document and smoothed the way for you: Susan Graham and John Addison, the official readers. Ricki Blau, although not an official reader, also took the time for a careful proofreading, for which I am very grateful.

I would also like to thank John Hennessy, Bob White, the Center for Integrated Systems, the Computer Systems Laboratory, and the Department of Electrical Engineering at Stanford University for providing me with the support, time, and facilities needed to complete this dissertation.

Then, there is the man who decided to take a RISC with Smalltalk and led the whole project (and me), challenged us to pull it off, challenged me to write it up, and went over this document with a fine-tooth comb, David Patterson.

Finally, let me thank my wife, Nina, and my parents for their love and moral support.

Bibliography

[AKW]   A. Aho, B. W. Kernighan and P. Weinberger, *Awk -- A Pattern Scanning and Processing Language*, Bell Laboratories, Murray Hill, NJ.

[Bad82] S. Baden, "High Performance Storage Reclamation in an Object-Based Memory System", Master's Report, Computer Science Division, Department of E.E.C.S, University of California, Berkeley, CA, June 9, 1982.

[Bak77] H. G. Baker, "List Processing in Real Time on a Serial Computer", A.I. Working Paper 139, MIT-AI Lab, Boston, MA, April, 1977.

[BaS83] S. Ballard and S. Shirron, "The Design and Implementation of VAX/Smalltalk-80", in *Smalltalk-80: Bits of History, Words of Advice*, G. Krasner (editor), Addison Wesley, 1983, 127-150.

[BGH82] J. Batali, E. Goodhue, C. Hanson, H. Shrobe, R. M. Stallman and G. J. Sussman, "The Scheme-81 Architecture–System and Chip", *Proceedings of the 1982 Conference on Advanced Research in VLSI*, Cambridge, MA, 1982.

[Bay84] "Dorado Benchmarks", *Smalltalk-80 Newsletter*, Palo Alto, CA, September 1984, 18.

[Bay85] "New Implementations Unveiled", *Smalltalk-80 Newsletter*, Palo Alto, CA, October 1985.

[BeF74] W. Becker and D. Fagen, "Throw Back the Little Ones", in *Throw Back the Little Ones*, Steely Dan, © American Broadcasting Music, Inc. (ASCAP), Los Angeles, CA, 1974.

[Bla83a]   J. Blakken, "Register Windows for SOAR", in *Smalltalk on a RISC: Architectural Investigations*, D. A. Patterson (editor), Computer Science Division, University of California, Berkeley, CA, April 1983, 126-140. Proceedings of CS292R.

[Bla83b]   R. Blau, "Paging on an Object-Oriented Personal Computer for Smalltalk", M.S. report and C.S. Division Technical Report, Computer Science Division, Department of E.E.C.S, University of California, Berkeley, CA, June, 1983.

[Bla83c]   R. Blau, "Tags and Traps for the SOAR Architecture", in *Smalltalk on a RISC: Architectural Investigations*, D. A. Patterson (editor), Computer Science Division, University of California, Berkeley, CA, April 1983, 24-41. Proceedings of CS292R.

[Bla83d]   R. Blau, "Paging on an Object-Oriented Personal Computer", *Proceedings of the ACM SIGMETRICS Conference on Measurement and Modeling of Computer Systems*, Minneapolis, MN, August, 1983.

[BlD83]   R. Blomseth and H. Davis, "The Orion Project -- A Home for SOAR", in *Smalltalk on a RISC: Architectural Investigations*, D. Patterson (editor), Computer Science Division, Deptartment of E.E.C.S., University of California, Berkeley, CA, April, 1983, 64-109.

[Bro84]   E. W. Brown, "A Virtual Memory CPU Board with a Large Cache", Master's Report, Computer Science Division, Department of E.E.C.S, University of California, Berkeley, CA, 1984.

[Bus85]   B. Bush, "Smalltalk-80 to SOAR Code", to be published as a Master's thesis, Computer Science Division, Department of E.E.C.S, University of California, Berkeley, CA, 1985.

[Cha82]   G. J. Chaitin, "Register Allocation and Spilling Via Graph Coloring", *Proceedings of the ACM SIGPLAN Notices' 82 Symposium on Compiler Construction*, 1982. SIGPLAN Notices Notices #17.

[Coh81]   J. Cohen, "Garbage collection of Linked Data Structures", *ACM Computing Surveys 13*, 3 (September 1981), 341-367.

[Col60]   G. E. Collins, "A Method for Overlapping and Erasure of Lists", *Comm. of the ACM 3*, 12 (December 1960), 655-657.

[DAmb83] B. D´Ambrosio, "Smalltalk-80 Language Measurements -- Dynamic Use of Compiled Methods", in *Smalltalk on a RISC: Architectural Investigations*, D. A. Patterson (editor), Computer Science Division, University of California, Berkeley, CA, April 1983, 110-125. Proceedings of CS292R.

[DMS84]   N. M. Delisle, D. E. Mencosy and M. D. Schwartz, "Viewing a Programming Environment as a Single Tool", *ACM Software Eng. Notes/SIGPLAN Notices Software Engineering Symposium on Practical Software Development Environments*, Pittsburgh, PA, April, 1984.

[Den70]   P. J. Denning, "Virtual Memory", *Computing Surveys 2*, 3 (September, 1970), 153-189.

[DeT80]   L. P. Deutch and E. A. Taft, editors. "Requirements for an Experimental Programming Environment", CSL-80-10, Xerox PARC, Palo Alto, California, 1980.

[DeB76]   L. P. Deutsch and D. G. Bobrow, "An Efficient Incremental Automatic Garbage Collector", *Comm. of the ACM 19*, 9 (September 1976), 522-526.

[Deu81]   L. P. Deutsch, Measurements of the Dorado Smaltalk-80 System, Berkeley Computer Systems Seminar, Fall, 1981.

[Deu82a]   L. P. Deutsch, Storage Reclamation, Berkeley Smalltalk Seminar, February 5, 1982.

[Deu82b]   L. P. Deutsch, An Upper Bound for Smalltalk-80 Execution on a Motorola 68000 CPU, Private communications, 1982.

[Deu83a]   L. P. Deutsch, *The Dorado Smalltalk-80 Implementation: Hardware Architecture's Impact on Software Architecture*, Addison Wesley, September, 1983.

[Deu83b]   L. P. Deutsch, Storage Management, Private communications, 1983.

[DeS84]   L. P. Deutsch and A. M. Schiffman, "Efficient Implementation of the Smalltalk-80 System", *Proceedings of the 11th Annual ACM SIGACT News-SIGPLAN Notices Symposium on the Principles of Programming Languages*, Salt Lake City, Utah, January, 1984.

[Deu85]   L. P. Deutsch, The Xerox 68000 Smalltalk-80 System, Private communications, 1985.

[Fat83]   R. Fateman, Garbage Collection Overhead, Private communcation, August, 1983.

[Feu72]   E. A. Feustel, "The Rice Research Computer–A tagged architecture", *AFIPS 40* (Spring, 1972), 369-377, AFIPS Press.

[FoF81]   J. K. Foderaro and R. J. Fateman, "Characterization of VAX Macsyma", *Proceedings of the 1981 ACM Symposium on Symbolic and Algebraic Computation*, Berkeley, CA, 1981, 14-19.

[Gol81]   A. Goldberg, "Introducing the Smalltalk-80 System", *Byte 6*, 8 (August 1981), 14-35.

[GoR83]   A. J. Goldberg and D. Robson, *Smalltalk-80: The Language and Its Implementation*, Addison-Wesley Publising Company, Reading, MA, 1983.

[Gol84]   A. Goldberg, *Smalltalk-80. The Interactive Programming Environment*, Addison-Wesley Publising Company, Reading, MA, 1984.

[HJB82]   J. Hennessy, N. Jouppi, F. Baskett, A. Strong, T. Gross, C. Rowen and J. Gill, "The MIPS Machine", *Proc. Compcon*, February 1982.

[HJP83]   J. L. Hennessy, N. P. Jouppi, S. Przybylski, C. Rowen and T. Gross, "Design of a High Performance VLSI Processor", *Third CalTech Conference on Very Large Scale Integration*, 1983.

[Ing83]   D. H. H. Ingalls, "The Evolution of the Smalltalk Virtual Machine", in *Smalltalk-80: Bits of History, Words of Advice*, G. Krasner (editor), Addison Wesley, 1983, 9-28.

[KaK83]   T. Kaehler and G. Krasner, "LOOM–Large Object-Oriented Memory for Smalltalk-80 Systems", in *Smalltalk-80: Bits of History, Words of Advice*, G. Krasner (editor), Addison-Wesley, Reading, MA, 1983, 249.

[KSP83]   M. G. H. Katevenis, R. W. Sherburne, D. A. Patterson and C. H. Séquin, "The RISC II Micro-Architecture", in *VLSI '83*, F. Anceau and E. J. Aas (editor), Elsevier Science Publishers (IFIP), North-Holland, 1983, 349-359.

[KEL62]   T. Kilburn, D. B. G. Edwards, M. J. Lanigan and F. H. Sumner, "One-Level Storage System", *IRE Transactions 2*, EC-11 (April 1962), 223-235. Also in *Computer Structures: Principles and Examples,* Daniel P. Siewiorek, C. Gordon Bell, and Allen Newell (editors). McGraw-Hill, New York, NY, 1982. 135-142.

[Knu73]   D. Knuth, *The Art of Computer Programming, Volume 1*, Addison-Wesley, Reading, MA, 1973.

[Kra83]   G. Krasner, ed., *Smalltalk-80: Bits of History, Words of Advice*, Addison Wesley, September, 1983.

[LPM81]   B. P. Lampson, K. A. Pier, G. A. McDaniel, S. M. Ornstein and D. W. Clark, "The Dorado: A High Performance Personal Computer", CSL-81-1, Xerox PARC, Palo Alto, California, January 1981.

[Lee84]   P. K. Lee, "The Design of a Debugger for SOAR", Master's thesis, Computer Science Division, Department of E.E.C.S, University of California, Berkeley, CA, September 1984.

[LiH83]   H. Lieberman and C. Hewitt, "A Real-Time Garbage Collector Based on the Lifetimes of Objects", *Comm. of the ACM 26*, 6 (June 1983), 419-429.

[LoK61]   W. Lonergan and P. King, "Design of the B 5500 System", *Datamation 7*, 5 (May 1961), 28-32. Also in *Computer Structures: Principles and Examples,* Daniel P. Siewiorek, C. Gordon Bell, and Allen Newell (editors), McGraw-Hill, New York, NY, 1982, 129-134.

[McC83] K. McCall, "The Smalltalk-80 Benchmarks", in *Smalltalk 80: Bits of History, Words of Advice*, G. Krasner (editor), Addison-Wesley, Reading, MA, 1983, 151-173.

[McC60] J. McCarthy, "Recursive Functions of Symbolic Expressions and Their Computation by Machine, I", *Comm. of the ACM 3* (1960), 184-195.

[MeC83] R. Meyers and D. Casseres, "An MC68000-Based Smalltalk-80 System", in *Smalltalk-80: Bits of History, Words of Advice*, G. Krasner (editor), Addison Wesley, 1983, 153-174.

[Moo85] D. A. Moon, "Architecture of the Symbolics 3600", *Twelfth Annual International Symposium on Computer Architecture*, Boston, MA, June, 1985, 76-83.

[MOSIS] *MOSIS (MOS Implementation System) User's Manual*, USC Information Sciences Institute, Marina Del Rey, CA.

[Org73] E. I. Organick, *Computer System Organization. The B5700/B6700 Series*, Academic Press, New York, NY, 1973.

[PaD80] D. A. Patterson and D. R. Ditzel, "The Case for the Reduced Instruction Set Computer", *Computer Architecture News 8*, 6 (15 October 1980), 25-33.

[PaS81] D. A. Patterson and C. H. Séquin, "RISC I: A Reduced Instruction Set VLSI Computer", *Proc. Eighth International Symposium on Computer Architecture*, Minneapolis, Minnesota, May 1981, 443-457.

[PaS82] D. A. Patterson and C. H. Séquin, "A VLSI RISC", *Computer 15*, 9 (September 1982), 8-21.

[Pen85a]   J. Pendleton, "Getting SOAR Off the Ground", Private communcation, Computer Science Division, Department of E.E.C.S, University of California, Berkeley, CA, October, 1985.

[Pen85b]   J. Pendleton, "A Design Methodology for VLSI Processors", Ph.D. dissertation, Department of E.E.C.S, University of California, Berkeley, CA, September, 1985.

[Pie83]   K. A. Pier, "A Retrospective on the Dorado, A High-Performance Personal Computer", *Proc. Tenth Annual Symposium on Computer Architecture*, Stockhom, Sweden, June, 1983, 252-269.

[Pon83a]   C. Ponder, "... but will RISC run LISP?? (a feasibility study)", Report No. UCB/CSD 83/122, Computer Science Division, Department of E.E.C.S, University of California, Berkeley, CA, August, 1983.

[Pon83b]   C. Ponder, *Performance Evaluation of the Symbolics 3600*, Computer Science Division, Department of E.E.C.S, University of California, Berkeley, CA, Spring, 1983. Informal report for CS 292R, High Level Language Computer Architecture.

[Rad82]   G. Radin, "The 801 Minicomputer", *Proc. Symposium on Architectural Support for Programming Languages and Operating Systems*, Palo Alto, California, March 1-3, 1982, 39-47.

[Roa83]   C. B. Roads, *3600 Technical Summary*, Symbolics, Inc., Cambridge, MA, 1983.

[Rov84]   P. Rovner, "On Adding Garbage Collection and Runtime Types to a Strongly-Typed, Statically-Checked, Concurrent Language", CSL-84-7, Xerox PARC, Palo Alto, California, 1984.

[SKF85]   A. D. Samples, M. Klein and P. Foley, "SOAR Architecture", Technical Report UCB/CS/85/226, Computer Science Division, Department of E.E.C.S, University of California, Berkeley, CA, March 1985. Unpublished, earlier version published as "Preliminary SOAR Architecture, Klein & Foley," in *Smalltalk on a RISC: Architectural Investigations, Proceedings of CS 292R.*.

[ScW67]   H. Schorr and W. M. Waite, "An Efficient Machine-Independant Procedure for Garbage Collection in Various List Structures", *Communications of the ACM 10*, 8 (August, 1967), 501-506.

[She83]   B. Sheil, "Environments for Exploratory Programming", *Datamation*, February, 1983.

[ShM83]   B. A. Sheil and L. Masinter, "Papers on Interlisp-D", Xerox technical report, CIS-5, Palo Alto, CA, 1983.

[Sta82]   J. W. Stamos, "A Large Object-Oriented Virtual Memory: Grouping Strategies, Measurements, and Performance", Xerox technical report, SCG-82-2, Xerox, Palo Alto Research Center, Palo Alto, CA, May 1982.

[Sta84]   J. W. Stamos, "Static Grouping of Small Objects to Enhance Performance of a Paged Virtual Memory", *ACM Transactions on Computer Systems 2*, 3 (May 1984), 155-180.

[Sta80]   T. A. Standish, *Data Structure Techniques*, Addison-Wesley, Reading, MA, 1980.

[SSS85]   *Sun-3 Architecture: A Sun Technical Report*, Sun Microsystems, Inc., September, 1985. preliminary edition.

[SHJ81]   G. J. Sussman, J. Holloway, G. L. S. Jr. and A. Bell, "Scheme-79–Lisp on a Chip", *Computer 14*, 7 (July, 1981), 10-21.

[SKA84]   N. Suzuki, K. Kubota and T. Aoki, "Sword 32: A Bytecode Emulating Microprocessor for Object-Oriented Languages", *Proceedings of the International Conference on Fifth Generation Computer Systems 1984*, Nov. 1984, 389-307.

[Suz84]   N. Suzuki, "Developing 32-Bit Smalltalk Processor With the Execution Rate of 1,400,000 Bytecode/Sec.", Unpublished, 1984. Translated from Japanese.

[SZH85]   D. C. Swinehart, P. T. Zellweger and R. B. Hagmann, "The Structure of Cedar", *Proceedings of the ACM SIGPLAN Notices 85 Symposium on Language Issues in Programming Environments*, Seattle, Washington, June, 1985.

[Tei69]   W. Teitelman, "Toward a Programming Laboratory", in *International Joint Conference on Artificial Intelligence*, D. Walker (editor), May, 1969.

[Tei72]   W. Teitelman, "Automated Programming—the Programmer's Assistant.", *Proceedings of the Fall Joint Computer Converence*, May 1972.

[Tei79]   W. Teitelman, "A Display Oriented Programmer's Assistant", *International Journal of Man-Machine Studies 11* (1979), 157-187.

[Tei83]   W. Teitelman, "The Cedar Programming Environment: A Midterm Report and Examination", CSL-83-11, Xerox PARC, Palo Alto, California, 1983.

[Tei84]   W. Teitelman, "A Tour Through Cedar", *IEEE Software 1*, 2 (April 1984), 44-73.

[Tha81]   A. J. Thadhani, "Interactive User Productivity", *IBM Systems Journal 20*, 4 (1981), 407-421.

[UnP83]   D. M. Ungar and D. A. Patterson, "Berkeley Smalltalk: Who Knows Where the Time Goes?", in *Smalltalk-80: Bits of History, Word of Advice*, G. Krasner (editor), Addison Wesley, 1983, 189-206.

[Ung84]   D. Ungar, "Generation Scavenging: A Non-Disruptive High Performance Storage Reclamation Algorithm", *ACM Software Eng. Notes/SIGPLAN Notices Software Engineering Symposium on Practical Software Development Environments*, Pittsburgh, PA, April 1984, 157-167.

[UBF84]   D. Ungar, R. Blau, P. Foley, D. Samples and D. Patterson, "Architecture of SOAR: Smalltalk on a RISC", *Eleventh Annual International Symposium on Computer Architecture*, Ann Arbor, MI, June, 1984, 188-197.

[Wal83]   D. Wallace, "Making Smalltalk less Becoming: Removing Primitive Becomes from Smalltalk-80", in *Smalltalk on a RISC: Architectural Investigations*, D. A. Patterson (editor), Computer Science Division, University of California, Berkeley, CA, April 1983, 213-222. Proceedings of CS292R.

[Weg71]   B. Wegbreit, "The ECL Programming System", *Procedings of the 19th AFIPS Fall Joint Computer Conference*, 1971, 253-262.

[Weg74]   B. Wegbreit, "The Treatment of Data Types in EL1", *Communications of the ACM 17*, 5 (May 1974), 251-264.

[Whi80]   J. L. White, "Address/Memory Management For A Gigantic LISP Environment or, GC Considered Harmful", *Conference Record of the 1980 LISP Conference*, Redwood Estates, CA, 1980, 119-127.

Appendix A

Detailed Performance Evaluation of Individual Features

A.1. Introduction

This appendix contains detailed evaluations of the effectiveness of most of the features in SOAR and a few proposed additions to SOAR. The raw data, instruction mixes, and execution time profiles on which these calculations are based are in Appendix B. To guide you through this section, we have reprinted part of the table of contents in Table A.1. There are two kinds of subroutines in SOAR: subroutines written by Xerox in Smalltalk, and subroutines written by us in assembler for runtime support. Since these are written in two different languages, they may have different instruction mixes. For this reason, our tables of dynamic data have three columns: one for the routines written in Smalltalk (ST), one for the routines written in assembler (system), and one that ignores the distinction (both). Since system code consumes two-thirds of the time, the averages (used in the other chapters) tend to be dominated by the behavior of the system code. If this code were optimized, the numbers for Smalltalk code would become more important for overall performance. For static measurements, the Smalltalk routines dwarf the assembler routines, and we usually omit the assembler ones.

A.2. Runtime Type Checking

Runtime type checking distinguishes Smalltalk-80 systems from those designed for conventional languages. SOAR supports this with a tag bit for integers and tagged integer arithmetic and comparison instructions.

Table A.1: Table of contents for Appendix A.

A.2.1. How Important are the Tagged Integer Instructions?

To support tagged integers, SOAR includes tagged versions of the arithmetic and comparison instructions. To assess their importance, we first measure their frequency of use, then calculate the performance degradation that would be caused by replacing them by equivalent software instructions.

A.2.1.1. Tagged Instruction Frequency

Table A.2 lists the frequency of each tagged integer instruction for several benchmarks. Zero rows have been omitted. Table A.2 above shows, for compiled Smalltalk-80 code, one out of every 8 instructions executed exploits SOAR's integer tag-checking hardware. Overall, the ratio is about 1 out of every 11 instructions. Interestingly, tagged skips outnumber tagged arithmetic in compiled code.

Another way to measure frequency is to count the static number of each kind of tagged instruction. Table A.3 shows that nearly 1 out of every 11 instructions is a tagged integer instruction. This is slightly lower than the dynamic frequency of 1 in 8.

How often does SOAR detect an integer tag trap? As Table A.4 shows, these traps are quite rare; less than 4 in 1,000 tagged instructions trap.

A.2.1.2. Cost of Omitting Tagged Arithmetic Instructions

How much slower would SOAR be without integer tag checking hardware? Table A.5 shows the sequences that would be needed without it, under the assumption that no compiler optimization is performed. (The feasibility of such optimization in the absence of type declarations has yet to be demonstrated.) Table A.6 summarizes these data with cost figures.

Table A.2: Frequency of tagged arithmetic instructions, Part 1.		
	ST	system	both
test3plus4			
all insts	65.14%	34.86%	100%
add	33.07%	0.00%	21.54%
trap1	0.00%	6.17%	2.15%
loadc	3.35%	0.06%	2.20%
total	36.42%	6.25%	25.89%
testActivationReturn			
all insts	97.21%	2.79%	100%
sub	9.46%	0.00%	9.20%
skip	9.46%	0.00%	9.20%
loadc	9.46%	0.00%	9.20%
total	28.40%	0.00%	27.61%
testClassOrganizer			
all insts	41.06%	58.94%	100%
add	1.19%	1.19%	1.19%
sub	0.34%	1.73%	1.15%
sll	0.00%	0.59%	0.35%
skip	2.26%	1.31%	1.70%
trap1	0.00%	2.49%	1.47%
load	0.00%	0.81%	0.81%
loadc	7.23%	0.10%	3.03%
total	11.03%	8.79%	9.71%
testCompiler			
all insts	33.42%	66.58%	100%
add	1.26%	0.89%	1.01%
sub	0.45%	1.17%	0.93%
sll	0.00%	0.29%	0.19%
skip	1.94%	0.87%	1.23%
trap1	0.00%	1.56%	1.04%
load	0.00%	1.02%	0.68%
loadc	7.30%	0.26%	2.60%
total	10.92%	6.07%	7.69%

Table A.2: Frequency of tagged arithmetic instructions, Part 2.

	ST	system	both
		testDecompiler	
all insts	32.19%	67.81%	100%
add	1.83%	1.00%	1.27%
sub	0.47%	1.17%	0.93%
and	0.09%	0.00%	0.03%
sll	0.00%	0.10%	0.07%
sra	0.00%	0.16%	0.11%
skip	2.52%	0.62%	1.23%
trap1	0.00%	1.56%	1.06%
load	0.00%	1.12%	0.76%
loadc	7.21%	0.28%	2.51%
total	12.08%	6.00%	7.95%
		testPrintDefinition	
all insts	38.01%	61.99%	100%
add	2.26%	1.37%	1.71%
sub	0.08%	2.69%	1.70%
skip	4.31%	0.02%	1.65%
trap1	0.00%	3.68%	2.28%
load	0.00%	2.56%	1.59%
loadc	7.97%	0.11%	3.10%
total	14.65%	10.44%	12.04%
		testPrintHierarchy	
all insts	26.25%	73.75%	100%
add	2.10%	0.26%	0.73%
sub	0.23%	0.84%	0.68%
skip	2.51%	0.05%	0.70%
trap1	0.00%	2.17%	1.60%
load	0.00%	1.45%	1.07%
loadc	7.62%	0.19%	2.14%
total	12.46%	4.98%	6.94%
		Average of macro-benchmarks	
all insts	34.19%	65.81%	100%
add	1.73%	0.94%	1.18%
sub	0.31%	1.52%	1.08%
and	0.02%	0.00%	0.01%
sll	0.00%	0.20%	0.12%
sra	0.00%	0.03%	0.02%
skip	2.71%	0.57%	1.30%
trap1	0.00%	2.29%	1.49%
load	0.00%	1.39%	0.98%
loadc	7.47%	0.19%	2.68%
total	12.23%	7.26%	8.87%

Table A.3: Static Occurrences of Tagged Integer Instructions In System.				
op	immediate?	count	code	code + data
add	yes	1066	0.63%	0.25%
add	no	1132	0.67%	0.26%
sub	yes	658	0.39%	0.15%
sub	no	868	0.51%	0.20%
and	yes	60	0.04%	0.01%
and	no	132	0.08%	0.03%
or	yes	2	0.00%	0.00%
or	no	22	0.01%	0.01%
skip	no	2668	1.58%	0.62%
loadc	yes	9254	5.49%	2.15%
total		15862	9.41%	3.69%

Table A.4: Frequency of integer tag traps, Part 1.
% of insts that tag trap

	ST	system	both
test3plus4			
instructions	65.14%	34.86%	100%
total	0.00%	0.00%	0.00%
testActivationReturn			
instructions	97.21%	2.79%	100%
total	0.00%	0.00%	0.00%
testClassOrganizer			
instructions	41.06%	58.94%	100%
skip	18.75%	0.00%	10.29%
loadc	25.39%	0.00%	24.90%
total	2.26%	0.00%	0.93%
testCompiler			
instructions	33.42%	66.58%	100%
skip	12.04%	0.02%	6.34%
loadc	15.41%	1.38%	14.52%
total	1.36%	0.00%	0.46%
testDecompiler			
instructions	32.19%	67.81%	100%
skip	4.99%	0.00%	3.28%
loadc	17.06%	0.16%	15.76%
total	1.35%	0.00%	0.44%
testPrintDefinition			
instructions	38.01%	61.99%	100%
skip	22.33%	0.00%	22.21%
loadc	1.03%	0.00%	1.01%
total	0.08%	0.00%	0.03%

Table A.4: Frequency of integer tag traps, Part 2.		
% of insts that tag trap		
ST	system	both
testPrintHierarchy		
instructions	26.25%	73.75%	100%
skip	2.20%	0.00%	2.07%
loadc	4.47%	0.00%	4.17%
total	0.40%	0.00%	0.10%
avg of all macro-benchmarks		
instructions	34.19%	65.81%	100%
skip	12.06%	0.00%	8.84%
loadc	12.67%	0.31%	12.07%
total	1.09%	0%	0.39%

Table A.5: Writearound for tagged instructions, Part 1.	
add & sub	
%or a, b, t;	(omit for immediate)
%skip ltu t, 1 << 31	
jump error	
%add/%sub a, b, c	
%xor a, b, t	
%and t, 1 << 31, t	
%skip ne t, 0;	(are signs equal?)
jump ok;	(no! is OK)
%xor a, c, t	
%and t, 1 << 31, t	
%skip eq t, 0;	(overflow?)
jump error	
and & or & xor	
%or	a, b, t; (ni only)
%skip ltu a, 1 << 31	
jump error	
%and/%or/%xor	
sll	
%skip ltu a, 1 << 31	
jump error	
%sll a, b,	
%xor a, b, t	
%and t, 1 << 31, t	
%skip eq t, 0;	(overflow?)
jump error	
srl	
%skip ltu a, 1 << 31	
jump error	
%srl a, b	
sra	
%skip ltu a, 1 << 31	
jump error	
%sra a, b	
%skip lt a, 1 << 30	
%or b, 1 << 30, b	

Table A.5: Writearound for tagged instructions, Part 2.

skip & trap	
%or a, b, t;	(omit for immediate)
%skip ltu a, 1 << 31	
jump error	
%sll a, ta;	(for 31-bit signed comparison only)
%sll b, tb;	(for 31-bit signed comparison only)
%skip/%trap cond ta, tb	
load imm & loadc	
%skip ltu a, 1 << 31	
jump error	
%load / %loadc (a)b, c	
load reg	
%xor a, b, t	
%skip geu t, 1 << 31	
jump error	
%load (a)b, c	

Table A.6: Cost summary by instruction.

op	static (words)	dynamic (cycles)
add	7-10	5-10*
sub	7-10	5-10*
and	2-3	2-3
or	2-3	2-3
xor	2-3	2-3
sll	6	6
srl	2	2
sra	4	4
skip	3-5	3-5
trap	3-5	3-5
load	2-3	2-3
loadc	2	2

The next step is to combine this cost data with the frequency data. Table A.7 lists the time cost of omitting each type of tagged instruction from SOAR. The benchmarks would take from 20% to 32% more time without integer tag checking hardware in SOAR.

---

* The wide variation is caused by the overflow check, which is faster for operands with opposite signs.

Table A.7: Time cost of omitting tagged integer instructions, Part 1.

	ST	system	both
test3plus4			
all cycles	59.51%	40.43%	100%
add	150.06%-300.12%	0.00%	89.40%-178.80%
trap1	0.00%	13.26%-22.11%	5.36%-8.94%
loadc	6.06%	0.10%	3.65%-3.65%
total	150.06%-330.12%	13.36%-22.21%	94.76%-187.74%
Performance relative to full SOAR (<100% is slower)			51%-35%
testActivationReturn			
all cycles	95.91%	4.09%	100%
sub	35.30%-70.65%	0.00%	33.87%-67.75%
skip	21.19%-35.31%	0.00%	20.32%-33.87%
loadc	14.13%	0.00%	13.55%
total	70.62%-120.08%	0.00%	67.74%-115.17%
Performance relative to full SOAR (<100% is slower)			60%-46%
testClassOrganizer			
all cycles	42.56%	57.44%	100%
add	3.99%-7.98%	4.27%-8.54%	4.15%-8.30%
sub	1.13%-2.26%	6.19%-12.38%	4.04%-8.08%
sll	0.00%	2.59%	1.49%
skip	4.61%-7.68%	2.80%-4.67%	3.57%-5.95%
trap1	0.00%	5.40%-8.98%	3.10%-5.16%
load	0.00%	1.98%-2.98%	1.14%-1.71%
loadc	9.80%	0.14%	4.25%-4.25%
total	19.54%-27.72%	23.38%-40.20%	21.74%-34.95%
Performance relative to full SOAR (<100% is slower)			82%-74%
testCompiler			
all cycles	34.07%	65.93%	100%
add	4.18%-8.35%	3.05%-6.11%	3.44%-6.87%
sub	1.52%-3.05%	4.06%-8.12%	3.20%-6.39%
and	0.03%-0.03%	0.00%-0.00%	0.01%-0.01%
sll	0.00%	1.17%	0.77%
sra	0.00%	0.02%	0.01%
skip	3.90%-6.49%	1.82%-3.02%	2.52%-4.20%
trap1	0.00%	3.22%-5.37%	2.12%-3.54%
load	0.00%	1.41%-2.12%	0.93%-1.40%
loadc	9.77%	0.35%	3.56%-3.56%
total	19.35%-27.65%	15.10%-26.28%	16.55%-26.74%
Performance relative to full SOAR (<100% is slower)			86%-79%

Table A.7: Time cost of omitting tagged integer instructions, Part 2.

	ST	system	both
		testDecompiler	
all cycles	32.38%	67.62%	100%
add	6.29%-12.58%	3.42%-6.85%	4.35%-8.70%
sub	1.55%-3.09%	4.00%-8.00%	3.20%-6.41%
and	0.09%-0.15%	0.00%	0.03%-0.05%
sll	0.00%	0.40%	0.27%
sra	0.00%	0.43%	0.29%
skip	5.13%-8.52%	1.29%-2.13%	2.53%-4.21%
trap1	0.00%	3.22%-5.37%	2.18%-3.63%
load	0.00%	1.54%-2.29%	1.04%-1.55%
loadc	9.82%	0.40%	3.44%-3.44%
total	22.86%-34.16%	14.68%-25.88%	17.34%-28.56%
Performance relative to full SOAR (<100% is slower)			85%-78%
		testPrintDefinition	
all cycles	38.09%	61.91%	100%
add	8.30%-16.61%	5.01%-10.02%	6.26%-12.53%
sub	0.25%-0.50%	9.89%-19.78%	6.22%-12.44%
skip	9.45%-15.78%	0.03%-0.05%	3.62%-6.04%
trap1	0.00%	8.09%-13.49%	5.01%-8.35%
load	0.00%	3.78%-5.65%	2.34%-3.50%
loadc	11.66%	0.16%	4.55%-4.55%
total	29.69%-44.55%	26.95%-49.16%	27.99%-47.40%
Performance relative to full SOAR (<100% is slower)			78%-68%
		testPrintHierarchy	
all cycles	25.90%	74.10%	100%
add	7.42%-14.85%	0.89%-1.78%	2.58%-5.16%
sub	0.82%-1.65%	2.95%-5.89%	2.40%-4.79%
and	0.04%	0.00%	0.01%
sll	0.00%	0.03%	0.02%
skip	5.37%-8.96%	0.12%-0.20%	1.48%-2.47%
trap1	0.00%	4.56%-7.60%	3.38%-5.63%
load	0.00%	2.04%-3.06%	1.51%-2.27%
loadc	10.89%	0.27%	3.02%-3.02%
total	24.52%-36.34%	10.84%-18.81%	14.38%-23.36%
Performance relative to full SOAR (<100% is slower)			87%-81%

Table A.7: Time cost of omitting tagged integer instructions, Part 3.

	ST	system	both
		average of macro-benchmarks	
all cycles	34.60%	65.40%	100%
add	6.04%-12.07%	3.33%-6.65%	4.15%-8.31%
sub	1.05%-2.11%	5.42%-10.84%	3.81%-7.62%
and	0.03%-0.04%	0.00%	0.01%-0.02%
sll	0.00%	0.84%	0.51%
sra	0.00%	0.09%	0.06%
skip	5.69%-9.49%	1.21%-2.01%	2.74%-4.57%
trap1	0%	4.9%-8.16%	3.16%-5.26%
load	0.00%	2.15%-3.22%	1.39%-2.09%
loadc	10.39%	0.26%	3.76%
total	23.19%-34.09%	18.19%-32.08%	19.61%-32.21%
Performance relative to full SOAR (<100% is slower)			84%-76%

Of course, eliminating tag checking hardware from SOAR would also incur a space cost for the extra checking instructions. Table A.8 combines the static cost data with the static frequency data to compute the code expansion resulting from omitting data tag checking hardware in SOAR. Again, we can ignore the

Table A.8: Static Cost of Omitting Tagged Arith Insts in System.
(3502 instruction words)
(493 data words)
(3995 total words in sys)
(168,581 SOAR words of compiled code & literals)
(4,600 Smalltalk subroutines)
(430,000 SOAR words total image)

op	immediate?	cost	%code	%code + data
add	yes	7462	4.42%	1.74%
add	no	11320	6.72%	2.64%
sub	yes	4606	2.73%	1.07%
sub	no	8680	5.15%	2.02%
and	yes	120	0.07%	0.03%
and	no	396	0.23%	0.09%
or	yes	4	0.00%	0.00%
or	no	66	0.04%	0.02%
skip	yes	0	0%	0%
skip	no	13340	7.91%	3.10%
loadc	yes	18508	10.98%	4.30%
total		64502	38.26%	15.00%

system code because it is so small. The data show that 38% more instructions would be needed — about 15% of the total image.

By moving the tag check into hardware we have increased the cost for a tag exception. SOAR must take a trap to handle one. The data show that only 0.39% of tagged instructions trap, and that only 12.5% of the instructions are tagged. Thus, a tag trap occurs once for every 2000 instructions. Since the tag trap handler prologue is about 25 instructions long, this represent a time cost of about 1.25%.

To summarize, SOAR without hardware support for integer tag checking and with the same code generation strategy would run 24% slower and require about 150 KB more memory.

A.2.2. Evaluating the Impact of Adding a Compare-and-Branch Instruction

Instead of condition codes, SOAR uses conditional skip instructions. This simplifies handling comparisons of data that are not integers. The tag trap handler need not set condition codes, but can merely return to the appropriate location. As a result, a conditional jump in SOAR takes two cycles: one for the skip instruction and another for the jump. This is as fast as it can be without an additional adder to compute jump addresses. If we had such a device how much faster could SOAR run? To bound the number of times a conditional jump instruction would be used we can count skips. We can find a more accurate figure by counting only those skips that skip over unconditional jumps. Table A.9 present these data. The table shows that the most that could be hoped for is an 8% improvement. Counting only those skips that follow jumps results in a time savings of 2.6%. The large disparity implies that there are many places where the conditionally executed code is only a single instruction.

Table A.9: Upper bound on speedup with compare-and-branch, Part 1.

	ST	system	both
testClassOrganizer			
instructions	41.06%	58.94%	100%
cycles	42.56%	57.44%	100%
untagged skip's per instruction	1.57%	12.39%	7.95%
tagged skip's per instruction	2.27%	1.30%	1.70%
total skip's per instruction	3.84%	13.69%	9.65%
skip-jumps per instruction	1.06%	5.49%	3.67%
untagged skip's per cycle	1.06%	8.91%	5.57%
tagged skip's per cycle	1.53%	0.93%	1.19%
total skip's per cycle	2.60%	9.84%	6.76%
skip-jumps per cycle	0.85%	4.43%	2.95%
testCompiler			
instructions	33.42%	66.58%	100%
cycles	34.07%	65.93%	100%
untagged skip's per instruction	1.50%	15.57%	10.87%
tagged skip's per instruction	1.93%	0.88%	1.23%
total skip's per instruction	3.44%	16.44%	12.10%
skip-jumps per instruction	1.37%	5.78%	4.30%
untagged skip's per cycle	1.01%	10.74%	7.42%
tagged skip's per cycle	1.30%	0.60%	0.84%
total skip's per cycle	2.30%	11.34%	8.26%
skip-jumps per cycle	0.92%	3.98%	2.94%
testDecompiler			
instructions	32.19%	67.81%	100%
cycles	32.38%	67.62%	100%
untagged skip's per instruction	0.72%	17.56%	12.14%
tagged skip's per instruction	2.51%	0.62%	1.23%
total skip's per instruction	3.23%	18.18%	13.37%
skip-jumps per instruction	1.29%	4.63%	3.56%
untagged skip's per cycle	0.49%	12.07%	8.32%
tagged skip's per cycle	1.71%	0.43%	0.84%
total skip's per cycle	2.20%	12.50%	9.16%
skip-jumps per cycle	0.88%	3.18%	2.44%

Table A.9: Upper bound on speedup with compare-and-branch, Part 2.

	ST	system	both
testPrintDefinition			
instructions	38.01%	61.99%	100%
cycles	38.09%	61.91%	100%
untagged skip's per instruction	1.38%	9.26%	6.26%
tagged skip's per instruction	4.32%	0.01%	1.65%
total skip's per instruction	5.69%	9.27%	7.91%
skip-jumps per instruction	1.45%	3.81%	2.91%
untagged skip's per cycle	1.01%	6.79%	4.58%
tagged skip's per cycle	3.15%	0.01%	1.21%
total skip's per cycle	4.16%	6.80%	5.79%
skip-jumps per cycle	1.06%	2.79%	2.13%
testPrintHierarchy			
instructions	26.25%	73.75%	100%
cycles	25.90%	74.10%	100%
untagged skip's per instruction	1.20%	14.73%	11.18%
tagged skip's per instruction	2.51%	0.06%	0.70%
total skip's per instruction	3.71%	14.78%	11.88%
skip-jumps per instruction	1.67%	3.90%	3.32%
untagged skip's per cycle	0.86%	10.33%	7.87%
tagged skip's per cycle	1.79%	0.04%	0.49%
total skip's per cycle	2.65%	10.37%	8.37%
skip-jumps per cycle	1.19%	2.74%	2.34%
average of macro-benchmarks			
instructions	34.19%	65.81%	100.00%
cycles	34.60%	65.40%	100.00%
untagged skip's per instruction	1.27%	13.90%	9.68%
tagged skip's per instruction	2.71%	0.57%	1.30%
total skip's per instruction	3.98%	14.47%	10.98%
skip-jumps per instruction	1.37%	4.72%	3.55%
untagged skip's per cycle	0.89%	9.77%	6.75%
tagged skip's per cycle	1.90%	0.40%	0.91%
total skip's per cycle	2.78%	10.17%	7.67%
skip-jumps per cycle	0.98%	3.42%	2.56%

For a static analysis, we counted the number of conditional jump sequences produced by the compiler (Table A.10). The table shows that little space would be saved.

A.2.3. Evaluating Two-Tone Instructions

SOAR has two modes of execution: tagged and untagged. Rather than putting a mode bit in the PSW and spending a cycle to switch modes when needed, we put a mode bit in each instruction. Table A.11 shows how much slower SOAR would run if it took extra time to switch modes. The table shows that SOAR would be 16% slower without two-tone instructions.

To compute the code expansion, we instrumented the compiler. Table A.12 analyzes these data. The table shows that the image would be 19% larger without two-tone instructions.

A.2.4. How Important Are Tagged Immediates?

SOAR's tagged immediate format crams tagged values such as **nil, true,** and **false** into a twelve-bit immediate field. Without this feature, a two-cycle load instruction would be needed to get a tagged value. Table A.13 analyzes the performance impact of this feature. For each benchmark, it gives the breakdown of cycles spent in Smalltalk vs. system code, then proceeds to give the percentage of immediates used requiring the tagged format, and finally, the time cost of

Table A.10: Space savings for compare-and-branch.	
conditional jumps	4734
image size	1,500 Kb
space savings for compare-and-branch	1.26%

Table A.11: Projected time cost of manipulating PSW mode bit.			
	ST	system	both
testClassOrganizer			
cycles	42.56%	57.44%	100%
cost of mode-setting instructions	17.86%	19.30%	18.69%
testCompiler			
cycles	34.07%	65.93%	100%
cost of mode-setting instructions	18.52%	12.68%	14.67%
testDecompiler			
cycles	32.38%	67.62%	100%
cost of mode-setting instructions	19.87%	11.92%	14.50%
testPrintDefinition			
cycles	38.09%	61.91%	100%
cost of mode-setting instructions	20.53%	20.35%	20.42%
testPrintHierarchy			
cycles	25.90%	74.10%	100%
cost of mode-setting instructions	21.74%	9.93%	12.99%
average of macro-benchmarks			
cycles	34.60%	65.40%	100.00%
cost of mode-setting instructions	19.70%	14.84%	16.25%

Table A.12: Space cost of mode bit in PSW.	
number of extra instructions to change PSW mode bit	70759
image size	1,500 kB
relative cost of PSW mode bit	18.87%

omitting this feature. These data suggest that SOAR would be 10% slower without this feature.

To analyze the impact of tagged immediates on the size of the compiled image, we instrumented our compiler (Table A.14). As expected, non-negative integers dominate immediate values. Pointer immediates are also frequent. Interestingly, boolean masks (all zeroes with a one in one of the top four bits, or tag values) provide a use for tagged immediates more often than pointers.

Table A.13: Dynamic usage and cost of tagged immediate values.
(All figures in percentages.)

	ST	system	both
testActivationReturn			
cycles	95.91%	4.09%	100%
tagged imms/all imms	9.09%	14.35%	9.29%
tagged imm cost/all cycles	7.06%	10.57%	7.21%
testClassOrganizer			
cycles	42.56%	57.44%	100%
tagged imms/all imms	14.96%	14.83%	14.86%
tagged imm cost/all cycles	6.59%	11.35%	9.32%
testCompiler			
cycles	34.07%	65.93%	100%
tagged imms/all imms	15.08%	15.89%	15.69%
tagged imm cost/all cycles	7.20%	11.94%	10.33%
testDecompiler			
cycles	32.38%	67.62%	100%
tagged imms/all imms	12.74%	16.77%	15.85%
tagged imm cost/all cycles	6.12%	13.01%	10.78%
testPrintDefinition			
cycles	38.09%	61.91%	100%
tagged imms/all imms	12.63%	10.29%	10.88%
tagged imm cost/all cycles	5.90%	8.75%	7.66%
testPrintHierarchy			
cycles	25.90%	74.10%	100%
tagged imms/all imms	11.33%	15.30%	14.61%
tagged imm cost/all cycles	5.29%	11.74%	10.07%
average of macro-benchmarks			
cycles	34.60%	65.40%	100.00%
tagged imms/all imms	13.35%	14.62%	14.38%
tagged imm cost/all cycles	6.22%	11.36%	9.63%

Table A.14: Raw data for static analysis of tagged immediates.

immediate value	count	OK in SOAR	OK w/o tagged immediates
non-negative integers	35106	yes	yes
negative 31-bit integers	7968	yes	yes*
boolean masks	2984	yes	no
pointers	2433	yes	no
invalid† pointers	8507	no	no
invalid† integers	868	no	yes*
total SOAR image size	1500 kB		

The next step is to count the number of immediates that would be unrepresentable without tagged immediates and determine the amount of further expansion in the image (Table A.15). Tagged immediates don't save much space; the image would only be 1.2% larger without them.

A.3. Interpretation

This section concerns features of SOAR's instruction set and trap system.

Table A.15: Impact of eliminating tagged immediates.

cost for pointers	5417 immediates
savings for integers	868 immediates
net cost	4549 immediates
relative cost	1.21%

---

* In order to be conservative, we assume that the negative immediates could be represented without tagged immediates by either changing the opcode to subtract instead of add or, for offsets, by using the full 32-bit representation. We further assume that the integers which are too big for our current scheme would fit in four more bits.

† These values do not fit in SOAR's tagged immediate format.

A.3.1. Evaluating SOAR's Byte Facilities

We perform two comparisons: the speedup possible with load/store byte instructions, and the slowdown had we not provided the insert and extract instructions. Table A.16 gives the important instruction sequences: LoadByte and storeByte are slightly faster than extract and insert, which in turn are much faster than relying on one bit shifts.

Next, in Table A.17 we gather frequency data on insert and extract instructions, and multiply by the various costs to evaluate the performance impact of these other two schemes. As shown in the last section of Table A.17, the average time savings for adding load/store byte instructions would be 7%, while the average time penalty for taking away the byte insert/extract instructions would

Table A.16: Codes sequences for byte operations, Part 1.		
(Byte 0 is least significant byte, byte 3 is most significant.)		
Loading a byte from memory		
	load byte instruction (addition to SOAR)	
loadByte	(base)offset + byteNo, dest	
time	2 cycles	
	extract byte instruction (current SOAR)	
load	(base)offset, dest	
extract	dest, byteNo, dest	
time	3 cycles	
	no special instructions (simplification to SOAR)	
load (base)offset, dest		
srl	dest, dest	(0 to 24 of these)
load	pcRel(mask), maskReg	(omit for byte 3)
and	dest, maskReg, dest	(omit for byte 3)
mask:	0xff	
byte 0 time	5 cycles	
byte 1 time	13 cycles	
byte 2 time	21 cycles	
byte 3 time	26 cycles	
avg. time	16 cycles	

Table A.16: Codes sequences for byte operations, Part 2.
(Byte 0 is least significant byte, byte 3 is most significant.)

	Storing a byte in memory	
	store byte instruction (addition to SOAR)	
storeByte	source, (base)offset + byteNo	
time	2 cycles	
	insert byte instruction (current SOAR)	
load	(base)offset, dest	
load	(base)offset, r1	
load	pcRel(mask), maskReg	
and	r1, maskReg, r1	
insert	source, byteNo, r2	
or	r1, r2, r1	
store	r1, (base)offset	
time	9 cycles	
	no special instructions (simplification of SOAR)	
load	(base)offset, r1	
load	pcRel(mask), maskReg	
and	r1, maskReg, r1	
sll	source, source	
xor	maskReg, -1, maskReg	(omit for byte 3)
and	source, maskReg, source	(omit for byte 3)
or	r1, source, r1	
store	r1, (base)offset	
byte 0 time	10 cycles	
byte 1 time	18 cycles	
byte 2 time	26 cycles	
byte 3 time	32 cycles	
avg. time	22 cycles	

Table A.17: Dynamic analysis of byte operations, Part 1.

testClassOrganizer			
steps	41.06%	58.94%	100%
cycles	42.56%	57.44%	100%
insert per inst	0	0.97%	0.57%
extract per inst	0	3.54%	2.09%
insert + extract per inst	0	4.51%	2.66%
insert per cycle	0	0.70%	0.40%
extract per cycle	0	2.54%	1.46%
insert + extract per cycle	0	3.24%	1.86%
store byte savings	0	4.87%	2.80%
load byte savings	0	2.54%	1.46%
load & store byte savings	0	7.41%	4.26%
min insert omission cost	0	0.70%	0.40%
min extract omission cost	0	5.09%	2.92%
min insert/extract omission cost	0	5.78%	3.32%
avg insert omission cost	0	9.04%	5.19%
avg extract omission cost	0	33.07%	18.99%
avg insert/extract omission cost	0	42.11%	24.19%
max insert omission cost	0	16.00%	9.19%
max extract omission cost	0	58.50%	33.60%
max insert/extract omission cost	0	74.50%	42.79%
testCompiler			
steps	33.42%	66.58%	100%
cycles	34.07%	65.93%	100%
insert per inst	0	0.75%	0.50%
extract per inst	0	2.62%	1.75%
insert + extract per inst	0	3.37%	2.24%
insert per cycle	0	0.52%	0.34%
extract per cycle	0	1.81%	1.19%
insert + extract per cycle	0	2.32%	1.53%
store byte savings	0	3.61%	2.38%
load byte savings	0	1.81%	1.19%
load & store byte savings	0	5.41%	3.57%
min insert omission cost	0	0.52%	0.34%
min extract omission cost	0	3.62%	2.38%
min insert/extract omission cost	0	4.13%	2.72%
avg insert omission cost	0	6.70%	4.41%
avg extract omission cost	0	23.51%	15.50%
avg insert/extract omission cost	0	30.20%	19.91%
max insert omission cost	0	11.85%	7.81%
max extract omission cost	0	41.59%	27.42%
max insert/extract omission cost	0	53.43%	35.23%

Table A.17: Dynamic analysis of byte operations, Part 2.

testDecompiler			
steps	32.19%	67.81%	100%
cycles	32.38%	67.62%	100%
insert per inst	0	1.12%	0.76%
extract per inst	0	2.77%	1.88%
insert + extract per inst	0	3.89%	2.64%
insert per cycle	0	0.77%	0.52%
extract per cycle	0	1.91%	1.29%
insert + extract per cycle	0	2.67%	1.81%
store byte savings	0	5.37%	3.63%
load byte savings	0	1.91%	1.29%
load & store byte savings	0	7.28%	4.92%
min insert omission cost	0	0.77%	0.52%
min extract omission cost	0	3.81%	2.58%
min insert/extract omission cost	0	4.58%	3.10%
avg insert omission cost	0	9.97%	6.74%
avg extract omission cost	0	24.78%	16.76%
avg insert/extract omission cost	0	34.75%	23.50%
max insert omission cost	0	17.65%	11.93%
max extract omission cost	0	43.84%	29.65%
max insert/extract omission cost	0	61.49%	41.58%
testPrintDefinition			
steps	38.01%	61.99%	100%
cycles	38.09%	61.91%	100%
insert per inst	0	2.23%	1.38%
extract per inst	0	6.03%	3.74%
insert + extract per inst	0	8.26%	5.12%
insert per cycle	0	1.63%	1.01%
extract per cycle	0	4.42%	2.74%
insert + extract per cycle	0	6.06%	3.75%
store byte savings	0	11.44%	7.08%
load byte savings	0	4.42%	2.74%
load & store byte savings	0	15.86%	9.82%
min insert omission cost	0	1.63%	1.01%
min extract omission cost	0	8.85%	5.48%
min insert/extract omission cost	0	10.48%	6.49%
avg insert omission cost	0	21.24%	13.15%
avg extract omission cost	0	57.51%	35.60%
avg insert/extract omission cost	0	78.75%	48.75%
max insert omission cost	0	37.57%	23.26%
max extract omission cost	0	101.75%	62.99%
max insert/extract omission cost	0	139.32%	86.25%

Table A.17: Dynamic analysis of byte operations, Part 3.

testPrintHierarchy			
steps	26.25%	73.75%	100%
cycles	25.90%	74.10%	100%
insert per inst	0	2.84%	2.09%
extract per inst	0	4.20%	3.10%
insert + extract per inst	0	7.04%	5.19%
insert per cycle	0	1.99%	1.47%
extract per cycle	0	2.95%	2.18%
insert + extract per cycle	0	4.94%	3.66%
store byte savings	0	13.93%	10.32%
load byte savings	0	2.95%	2.18%
load & store byte savings	0	16.88%	12.51%
min insert omission cost	0	1.99%	1.47%
min extract omission cost	0	5.89%	4.37%
min insert/extract omission cost	0	7.88%	5.84%
avg insert omission cost	0	25.87%	19.17%
avg extract omission cost	0	38.30%	28.38%
avg insert/extract omission cost	0	64.17%	47.55%
max insert omission cost	0	45.77%	33.92%
max extract omission cost	0	67.76%	50.21%
max insert/extract omission cost	0	113.54%	84.13%
average of macro-benchmarks			
steps	34.19%	65.81%	100.00%
cycles	34.60%	65.40%	100.00%
insert per inst	0.00%	1.58%	1.06%
extract per inst	0.00%	3.83%	2.51%
insert + extract per inst	0.00%	5.41%	3.57%
insert per cycle	0.00%	1.12%	0.75%
extract per cycle	0.00%	2.73%	1.77%
insert + extract per cycle	0.00%	3.85%	2.52%
store byte savings	0.00%	7.84%	5.24%
load byte savings	0.00%	2.73%	1.77%
load & store byte savings	0.00%	10.57%	7.02%
min insert omission cost	0.00%	1.12%	0.75%
min extract omission cost	0.00%	5.45%	3.55%
min insert/extract omission cost	0.00%	6.57%	4.29%
avg insert omission cost	0.00%	14.56%	9.73%
avg extract omission cost	0.00%	35.43%	23.05%
avg insert/extract omission cost	0.00%	50.00%	32.78%
max extract omission cost	0.00%	62.69%	40.77%
max insert omission cost	0.00%	25.77%	17.22%
max insert/extract omission cost	0.00%	88.46%	58.00%

be 33%. Byte insert/extract instructions seem to be a good compromise between functionality and efficiency.

A.3.2. Evaluation of the loadc instruction

Is loadc necessary? Loadc is a load instruction with a different opcode that is only used to obtain the class (data type) of an object. If the object is an integer, the resulting trap can be handled faster because the reason for the trap as well as the destination register are fixed by convention. However, the trap handler for the ordinary load instruction could discover an attempt to access the class field by merely testing for an offset of zero. It would take only two more cycles to test the offset value (in a shadow register) and branch. Table A.18 contains an analysis of this performance impact based on the frequency of loadc traps. The table shows that SOAR could function quite well without loadc. At worst, SOAR would be only 1% slower without it.

A.3.3. Barrel Shifter

Many VLSI processors have included a barrel shifter to perform multi-bit shifts in a single cycle. SOAR lacks this feature. Although undisputably important for BitBLT, we thought that multiple-bit shifts would not be needed for Smalltalk-80 code per se. To confirm this, we instrumented our simulator to detect consecutive cascaded shift operations and total the second through last. This reflects the savings a barrel shifter would realize. Table A.19 has this data. These data show that a barrel shifter would not help out SOAR.

A.3.4. Evaluating the importance of Multiply and Divide

SOAR provides no help for multiplication or division. Is this a mistake? The only place Smalltalk-80 uses these operations is runtime support routines for integers. We ran the benchmarks and sampled the program counter to generate

Table A.18: Loadc Time Analysis, Part 1.

(All numbers are in percents.)

benchmark	Smalltalk	system	both
testActivationReturn			
steps	97.21%	2.79%	100%
cycles	95.91%	4.09%	100%
loadc per inst	9.47%	0.01%	9.20%
loadc per cycle	7.06%	0.01%	6.77%
loadc traps per loadc	0%	0%	0%
cost of omitting loadc	0%	0%	0%
testClassOrganizer			
steps	41.06%	58.94%	100%
cycles	42.56%	57.44%	100%
loadc per inst	7.24%	0.10%	3.03%
loadc per cycle	4.90%	0.07%	2.13%
loadc traps per loadc	25.39%	0%	24.90%
cost of omitting loadc	2.49%	0%	1.06%
testCompiler			
steps	33.42%	66.58%	100%
cycles	34.07%	65.93%	100%
loadc per inst	7.29%	0.25%	2.60%
loadc per cycle	4.89%	0.17%	1.78%
loadc traps per loadc	15.41%	1.38%	14.52%
cost of omitting loadc	1.51%	0.00%	0.52%
testDecompiler			
steps	32.19%	67.81%	100%
cycles	32.38%	67.62%	100%
loadc per inst	7.20%	0.29%	2.51%
loadc per cycle	4.91%	0.20%	1.72%
loadc traps per loadc	17.06%	0.16%	15.76%
cost of omitting loadc	1.67%	0.00%	0.54%
testPrintDefinition			
steps	38.01%	61.99%	100%
cycles	38.09%	61.91%	100%
loadc per inst	7.98%	0.11%	3.10%
loadc per cycle	5.83%	0.08%	2.27%
loadc traps per loadc	1.03%	0%	1.01%
cost of omitting loadc	0.12%	0%	0.05%
testPrintHierarchy			
steps	26.25%	73.75%	100%
cycles	25.90%	74.10%	100%
loadc per inst	7.62%	0.19%	2.14%
loadc per cycle	5.44%	0.13%	1.51%
loadc traps per loadc	4.47%	0%	4.17%
cost of omitting loadc	0.49%	0%	0.13%

Table A.18: Loadc Time Analysis, Part 2.
(All numbers are in percents.)

benchmark	smalltalk	system	both
average of macro-benchmarks			
steps	34.19%	65.81%	100.00%
cycles	34.60%	65.40%	100.00%
loadc per inst	7.47%	0.19%	2.68%
loadc per cycle	5.19%	0.13%	1.88%
loadc traps per loadc	12.67%	0.31%	12.07%
cost of omitting loadc	1.26%	0.00%	0.46%

Table A.19: Performance improvement of adding a barrel shifter.

	ST	system	both
testClassOrganizer			
cycles	42.56%	57.44%	100%
savings on sll's	0	0	0
savings on srl's	0	0.69%	0.40%
savings on sra's	0	0	0
total savings	0	0.69%	0.40%
testCompiler			
cycles	34.07%	65.93%	100%
savings on sll's	0	0.00%	0.00%
savings on srl's	0	0.26%	0.17%
savings on sra's	0	0.00%	0.00%
total savings	0	0.27%	0.18%
testDecompiler			
cycles	32.38%	67.62%	100%
savings on sll's	0	0	0
savings on srl's	0	0.23%	0.15%
savings on sra's	0	0	0
total savings	0	0.23%	0.15%
testPrintDefinition			
cycles	38.09%	61.91%	100%
savings on sll's	0	0	0
savings on srl's	0	0.95%	0.59%
savings on sra's	0	0	0
total savings	0	0.95%	0.59%
testPrintHierarchy			
cycles	25.90%	74.10%	100%
savings on sll's	0	0	0
savings on srl's	0	0.74%	0.55%
savings on sra's	0	0	0
total savings	0	0.74%	0.55%
average of macro-benchmarks			
cycles	34.60%	65.40%	100.00%
savings on sll's	0.00%	0.00%	0.00%
savings on sra's	0.00%	0.00%	0.00%
savings on srl's	0.00%	0.57%	0.37%
total savings	0.00%	0.58%	0.37%

execution profiles. Table A.20 shows the results for the multiply and divide routines. The table shows that the average time spent in these routines is 3.2%. Extra hardware for these operations would have had little performance impact.

Table A.20: Time spent in multiply and divide routines.			
benchmark	multiply	divide	total
testClassOrganizer	3.2%	5.2%	8.4%
testCompiler	1.7%	3.0%	4.7%
testDecompiler	0.9%	2.1%	3.0%
testPrintDefinition	0.0%	0.0%	0.0%
testPrintHierarchy	0.0%	0.0%	0.0%
average	1.2%	2.1%	3.2%

A.3.5. Evaluating the In1/Out1 Skip Condition

Table A.21 presents an analysis of the cost of omitting this condition from SOAR's instruction set. We assume that the cost of simulating this operation is two cycles: one to decrement each operand. This is an insignificant feature.

A.3.6. Evaluating SOAR's Conditional Trap Instruction

Conditional trap instructions can save one cycle for a comparison whose outcome can be predicted. Our SOAR software exploits the trap instruction to verify the in-line procedure call cache, to check the tags of return values, and to test the types of arguments to primitive routines. Table A.22 shows the sequence that would be required without this instruction. Table A.23 shows the trap instruction dynamic frequency, and the time cost for omitting this feature from SOAR. Since the overhead is one cycle per trap instruction, the difference between the two numbers arises because the average instruction duration is 1.5 cycles. The data show that SOAR would be 4% slower without this feature.

To analyze the impact of eliminating trap instructions on the size of the compiled image, we instrumented our compiler to count trap instructions. Then assuming that each such instruction would become two instructions — a skip followed by a call — we can calculate the total impact (Table A.24).

Table A.21: Analysis of In1/Out1 condition.

	ST	system	both
testClassOrganizer			
instructions	41.06%	58.94%	100%
cycles	42.56%	57.44%	100%
in1/out1 uses per inst	0%	0%	0%
cost of omitting in1/out1%	0%	0%	0%
testCompiler			
instructions	33.42%	66.58%	100%
cycles	34.07%	65.93%	100%
in1/out1 uses per inst	0%	0.00%	0.00%
cost of omitting in1/out1%	0%	0.00%	0.00%
testDecompiler			
instructions	32.19%	67.81%	100%
cycles	32.38%	67.62%	100%
in1/out1 uses per inst	0%	0.04%	0.03%
cost of omitting in1/out1%	0%	0.03%	0.02%
testPrintDefinition			
instructions	38.01%	61.99%	100%
cycles	38.09%	61.91%	100%
in1/out1 uses per inst	0%	0%	0%
cost of omitting in1/out1%	0%	0%	0%
testPrintHierarchy			
instructions	26.25%	73.75%	100%
cycles	25.90%	74.10%	100%
in1/out1 uses per inst	0%	0.00%	0.00%
cost of omitting in1/out1%	0%	0.00%	0.00%

Table A.22: Writearound for trap instruction.

skip	
call	
Extra Cost	1 cycle

Table A.23: Time cost of omitting the trap instruction.			
(All numbers are percentages.)			
	ST	sys	both
testActivationReturn			
instructions	97.21%	2.79%	100%
cycles	95.91%	4.09%	100%
trap instructions per instruction	14.20%	0.02%	13.80%
cost w/o trap instruction	10.59%	0.01%	10.16%
testClassOrganizer			
instructions	41.06%	58.94%	100%
cycles	42.56%	57.44%	100%
trap instructions per instruction	9.53%	3.53%	5.99%
cost w/o trap instruction	6.44%	2.54%	4.20%
testCompiler			
instructions	33.42%	66.58%	100%
cycles	34.07%	65.93%	100%
trap instructions per instruction	9.38%	2.35%	4.70%
cost w/o trap instruction	6.28%	1.62%	3.21%
testDecompiler			
instructions	32.19%	67.81%	100%
cycles	32.38%	67.62%	100%
trap instructions per instruction	9.31%	2.51%	4.70%
cost w/o trap instruction	6.35%	1.73%	3.22%
testPrintDefinition			
instructions	38.01%	61.99%	100%
cycles	38.09%	61.91%	100%
trap instructions per instruction	9.35%	5.64%	7.05%
cost w/o trap instruction	6.83%	4.13%	5.16%
testPrintHierarchy			
instructions	26.25%	73.75%	100%
cycles	25.90%	74.10%	100%
trap instructions per instruction	9.07%	4.22%	5.49%
cost w/o trap instruction	6.48%	2.96%	3.87%
average of macro-benchmarks			
instructions	34.19%	65.81%	100.00%
cycles	34.60%	65.40%	100.00%
trap instructions per instruction	9.33%	3.65%	5.59%
cost w/o trap instruction	6.48%	2.60%	3.93%

Table A.24: Raw data for static analysis of trap instructions.	
total number of trap instructions	7638
total SOAR image size	1500 kB
relative size impact	2.04%

Trap instructions improve image size even less than execution speed, and our image would only be 2% larger without them.

A.3.7. One-Cycle Traps

At one point in the design of SOAR, we decided to extend the trap operation rather than lengthen the cycle time [Pen85b]. This resulted in two-cycle traps instead of one-cycle traps. How many cycles did this decision cost us? Table A.25 presents our data. The result of adding the extra cycle to the trap operation was to require fewer than one percent more cycles. This was a good decision.

A.3.8. Evaluating the Performance Impact of Shadow Registers

To ascertain the time cost of omitting shadow registers from SOAR, we measured the frequencies of the various types of traps, estimated the added cost of handling each type without shadow registers, and multiplied the two together. One trap we could not measure was the page fault trap. Handling a page fault takes so long though, that the few cycles saved by shadow registers will not make much difference. The traps we did include were: integer tag traps (TT) on ALU and load/store instructions, register window overflows (WO) on call instructions, register window underflows (WU) on return instructions, traps cause by conditional trap instructions (TI), and Generation Scavenge traps (GS) on store instructions. Of these, only tag and Generation Scavenge trap handlers profit from the shadow registers. Table A.26 summarizes our results.

Table A.25: Trap frequencies, Part 1.		
	ST	system	both
classOrganizer			
cycles	42.56%	57.44%	100%
TT's per cycle	1.53%	0.00%	0.65%
WO's per cycle	0.53%	0.05%	0.23%
WU's per cycle	0.43%	0.13%	0.18%
TI's per cycle	0.05%	0.00%	0.02%
total traps per cycle	2.54%	0.18%	1.08%
compiler			
cycles	34.07%	65.93%	100%
TT's per cycle	0.91%	0.00%	0.31%
WO's per cycle	0.56%	0.09%	0.19%
WU's per cycle	0.51%	0.12%	0.17%
TI's per cycle	0.24%	0.01%	0.08%
GS's per cycle	0.00%	0.02%	0.00%
total traps per cycle	2.22%	0.24%	0.76%
decompiler			
cycles	32.38%	67.62%	100%
TT's per cycle	0.92%	0.00%	0.30%
WO's per cycle	0.34%	0.08%	0.11%
WU's per cycle	0.37%	0.07%	0.12%
TI's per cycle	0.34%	0.00%	0.11%
total traps per cycle	1.98%	0.15%	0.64%
printDefinition			
cycles	38.09%	61.91%	100%
TT's per cycle	0.76%	0.00%	0.29%
WO's per cycle	0.04%	0.02%	0.01%
WU's per cycle	0.05%	0.02%	0.02%
TI's per cycle	0.04%	0.00%	0.02%
GS's per cycle	0.01%	0.00%	0.00%
total traps per cycle	0.90%	0.03%	0.34%
printHierarchy			
cycles	25.90%	74.10%	100%
TT's per cycle	0.28%	0.00%	0.07%
WO's per cycle	0.38%	0.03%	0.10%
WU's per cycle	0.27%	0.07%	0.07%
TI's per cycle	0.28%	0.00%	0.07%
GS's per cycle	0.08%	0.00%	0.02%
total traps per cycle	1.29%	0.10%	0.33%

Table A.25: Trap frequencies, Part 2.

	ST	system	both
average of macro-benchmarks			
cycles	0.00%	0.00%	100.00%
TT's per cycle	0.88%	0.00%	0.32%
WO's per cycle	0.37%	0.05%	0.13%
WU's per cycle	0.33%	0.08%	0.11%
TI's per cycle	0.19%	0.00%	0.06%
GS's per cycle	0.02%	0.00%	0.00%
total traps per cycle	1.79%	0.14%	0.63%

Table A.26: Time cost of omitting shadow registers.
(All figures in percents.)

	ST	system	both
testActivationReturn			
cycles	95.91%	4.09%	100%
shadow cost for GS	0%	0%	0%
shadow cost for TT	0%	0%	0%
shadow cost for both	0%	0%	0%
testClassOrganizer			
cycles	42.56%	57.44%	100%
shadow cost for GS	0.00%	0%	0.00%
shadow cost for TT	0.12%	0%	0.05%
shadow cost for both	0.12%	0%	0.05%
testCompiler			
cycles	34.07%	65.93%	100%
shadow cost for GS	0.00%	0.01%	0.00%
shadow cost for TT	0.07%	0%	0.02%
shadow cost for both	0.07%	0.01%	0.03%
testDecompiler			
cycles	32.38%	67.62%	100%
shadow cost for GS	0%	0%	0%
shadow cost for TT	0.04%	0%	0.01%
shadow cost for both	0.04%	0%	0.01%
testPrintDefinition			
cycles	38.09%	61.91%	100%
shadow cost for GS	0.00%	0%	0.00%
shadow cost for TT	0.30%	0%	0.12%
shadow cost for both	0.30%	0%	0.12%
testPrintHierarchy			
cycles	25.90%	74.10%	100%
shadow cost for GS	0.02%	0%	0.01%
shadow cost for TT	0.02%	0%	0.00%
shadow cost for both	0.04%	0%	0.01%
average of macro-benchmarks			
cycles	34.60%	65.40%	100.00%
shadow cost for GS	0.00%	0.00%	0.00%
shadow cost for TT	0.11%	0.00%	0.04%
shadow cost for both	0.11%	0.00%	0.04%

These data seem to suggest that shadow registers do not significantly improve performance. The maximum improvement is 0.12%.

A.3.9. Does SOAR Really Need Vectored Traps?

Suppose the reason for a trap appeared in the PSW register. Then, the instructions in Table A.27 would simulate the effect of vectored traps. As the table shows, the cost would be four more cycles per trap.

We can then estimate the overall performance impact by counting the number of traps that occur (Table A.28). Since this would presumably allow us to shorten our traps by a cycle, the table also lists the cost of the extra trap cycle in the current SOAR system. The table indicates that the new effect of non-vectored traps would be a 2.2% percent time penalty.

A.4. Procedure Calls

Next we examine SOAR's features that help procedure calls.

A.4.1. Evaluating SOAR's Register File Organization

Unlike other RISCs, the chips designed at Berkeley feature multiple overlapping on-chip register windows. These reduce the amount of saving and restoring for calls and returns. If this feature were left out of SOAR, then each call would have to save the registers it needed, and each return would have to restore

Table A.27: Simulating vectored traps.	
%jump	
%extract	psw, 2, r_temp
%ret	
(jump table)	
Extra Cost	4 cycles

Table A.28: Time cost of non-vectored traps, Part 1.

	Smalltalk	System	both
testActivationReturn			
instructions	97.21%	2.79%	100%
time	95.91%	4.09%	100%
traps per instruction	0.30%	0.02%	0.29%
cost of extra trap cycle/all cycles	0.22%	0.01%	0.21%
cost of nonvectored traps/all cycles	0.89%	0.04%	0.85%
testClassOrganizer			
instructions	41.06%	58.94%	100%
time	42.56%	57.44%	100%
traps per instruction	3.75%	0.25%	1.69%
cost of extra trap cycle/all cycles	2.54%	0.18%	1.18%
cost of nonvectored traps/all cycles	10.14%	0.72%	4.73%
testCompiler			
instructions	33.42%	66.58%	100%
time	34.07%	65.93%	100%
traps per instruction	3.31%	0.35%	1.34%
cost of extra trap cycle/all cycles	2.22%	0.24%	0.92%
cost of nonvectored traps/all cycles	8.88%	0.97%	3.66%
testDecompiler			
instructions	32.19%	67.81%	100%
time	32.38%	67.62%	100%
traps per instruction	2.90%	0.22%	1.08%
cost of extra trap cycle/all cycles	1.98%	0.15%	0.74%
cost of nonvectored traps/all cycles	7.90%	0.59%	2.96%
testPrintDefinition			
instructions	38.01%	61.99%	100%
time	38.09%	61.91%	100%
traps per instruction	1.23%	0.05%	0.50%
cost of extra trap cycle/all cycles	0.90%	0.03%	0.36%
cost of nonvectored traps/all cycles	3.60%	0.14%	1.46%
testPrintHierarchy			
instructions	26.25%	73.75%	100%
time	25.90%	74.10%	100%
traps per instruction	1.81%	0.15%	0.58%
cost of extra trap cycle/all cycles	1.29%	0.10%	0.41%
cost of nonvectored traps/all cycles	5.16%	0.42%	1.65%

Table A.28: Time cost of non-vectored traps, Part 2.			
	Smalltalk	System	both
average of macro-benchmarks			
instructions	34.19%	65.81%	100.00%
time	34.60%	65.40%	100.00%
traps per instruction	2.60%	0.20%	1.04%
cost of extra trap cycle/all cycles	1.79%	0.14%	0.72%
cost of nonvectored traps/all cycles	7.14%	0.57%	2.89%

the saved registers. To measure this hypothetical cost, assuming no compiler optimization, we counted the number of non-nil registers before each return instruction. This count of modified registers was then doubled to account for both the saving and restoring cost. Finally, we added two cycles per return to account for the extra cycle of the loadm and storem instructions. Table A.29 presents these data. SOAR's multiple register windows are the most significant architectural feature on the chip: The benchmarks would take 70% more time without them.

How much would the image expand without register windows? The cost would be two instructions upon entering a subroutine (a subtract to adjust a stack pointer and a storem to save registers), and two instructions for each return from the routine (a loadm to restore the registers and an add to restore the sp). Table A.30 gives our analysis.

A.4.2. Number of Registers per Window

With only eight registers, SOAR's windows are much smaller than RISC II's. Measurements of Berkeley Smalltalk suggested that this would be sufficient. To verify this we instrumented our system and ran some benchmarks. When more registers are needed for a subroutine, it allocates a *spill* area in main memory. Thus, we merely counted the number of spill objects allocated and divided by the total number of calls. Also, we measured how many words were spilled to determine how many more registers were needed. Table A.31 presents

Table A.29: Analysis of register windows, Part 1.			
	ST	sys	both
testActivationReturn			
instructions	97.21%	2.79%	100%
cycles	95.91%	4.09%	100%
retw's* / all insts	9.62%	0.06%	9.35%
retw's* / cycles	7.17%	0.03%	6.88%
avg regs used / retw*	3.98	5.17	4.98
cost of saving & restoring regs/all cycles	71.52%	0.37%	82.38%
cost of WO/U			4%
net cost of no reg file			78.38%
perf vs full SOAR			56.06%
testClassOrganizer			
instructions	41.06%	58.94%	100%
cycles	42.56%	57.44%	100%
retw's* / all insts	9.78%	4.62%	6.74%
retw's* / cycles	6.61%	3.32%	4.72%
avg regs used / retw*	3.53	5.00	5.12
cost of saving & restoring regs/all cycles	59.90%	39.85%	57.83%
cost of WO/U			9.80%
net cost of no reg file			48.03%
perf vs full SOAR			67.55%
testCompiler			
instructions	33.42%	66.58%	100%
cycles	34.07%	65.93%	100%
retw's* / all insts	9.64%	3.82%	5.77%
retw's* / cycles	6.46%	2.64%	3.94%
avg regs used / retw*	3.62	5.26	5.35
cost of saving & restoring regs/all cycles	59.75%	33.00%	49.99%
cost of WO/U			9.50%
net cost of no reg file			40.49%
perf vs full SOAR			71.18%

Table A.29: Analysis of register windows, Part 2.

	ST	sys	both
testDecompiler			
instructions	32.19%	67.81%	100%
cycles	32.38%	67.62%	100%
retw's* / all insts	8.76%	3.62%	5.27%
retw's* / cycles	5.97%	2.49%	3.62%
avg regs used / retw*	3.78	5.42	5.54
cost of saving & restoring regs/all cycles	57.11%	31.93%	47.31%
cost of WO/U			6.40%
net cost of no reg file			40.91%
perf vs full SOAR			70.97%
testPrintDefinition			
instructions	38.01%	61.99%	100%
cycles	38.09%	61.91%	100%
retw's* / all insts	8.19%	5.52%	6.53%
retw's* / cycles	5.98%	4.04%	4.78%
avg regs used / retw*	3.69	5.27	5.52
cost of saving & restoring regs/all cycles	56.17%	50.69%	62.35%
cost of WO/U			0.50%
net cost of no reg file			61.85%
perf vs full SOAR			61.79%
testPrintHierarchy			
instructions	26.25%	73.75%	100%
cycles	25.90%	74.10%	100%
retw's* / all insts	8.68%	2.79%	4.33%
retw's* / cycles	6.20%	1.95%	3.05%
avg regs used / retw*	4.01	5.98	5.94
cost of saving & restoring regs/all cycles	62.11%	27.27%	42.40%
cost of WO/U			5.10%
net cost of no reg file			37.30%
perf vs full SOAR			72.83%
average of macro-benchmarks			
instructions	34.19%	65.81%	100.00%
cycles	34.60%	65.40%	100.00%
retw's* / all insts	9.01%	4.07%	5.73%
retw's* / cycles	6.24%	2.89%	4.02%
avg regs used / retw*	3.73	5.39	5.49
cost of saving & restoring regs/all cycles	59.01%	36.55%	51.98%
cost of WO/U			6.26%
net cost of no reg file			45.72%
perf vs full SOAR			68.86%

* includes all return instructions that change register windows: retw, retiw, retnw, retinwk — tagged or untagged.

Table A.30: Static analysis of register windows.	
routine entry points	4654
routine exit points	6795
image size	1500 kB
relative cost	6.11%

these data. These data show that SOAR's windows are large enough for Smalltalk-80 programs; more than 97% of the subroutines called fit into a window.

Table A.31: Spill area analysis.	
testCompiler	
total number of cycles	~1,100,000
total number of Smalltalk calls	~18,000
number of calls using spill area	430
total size of spill areas actually needed	883
avg. words of spill area used	2.1
fraction of calls needing spill areas	2.3%
mean number of cycles per spill allocation	2,600
testDecompiler	
total number of cycles	~2,900,000
total number of Smalltalk calls	~46,000
number of calls using spill area	1085
total size of spill areas actually needed	2807
avg. words of spill area used	2.6
fraction of calls needing spill areas	2.4%
mean number of cycles per spill allocation	2,700

A.4.3. Analysis of Loadm & Storem

The first step in evaluating the impact of the load- and store- multiple instructions is to measure their frequency. Since the time to simulate one of these instructions depends on the number of registers actually accessed, we also gathered those data (Table A.32). The loadm and storem instructions rarely occur, only one in 130 instructions.

Table A.32: Loadm/storem execution frequencies, Part 1.		
	ST	SYS	both
testActivationReturn			
instructions	97.21%	2.79%	100%
loadms per instruction	0.00%	5.19%	0.14%
loadms w/ 8 regs	0.00%	100.00%	100.00%
mean loadm regs	0	8	8
storems per instruction	0.00%	5.19%	0.14%
storems w/ 8 regs	0.00%	100.00%	100.00%
mean storem regs	0	8	8
testClassOrganizer			
instructions	41.06%	58.94%	100%
loadms per instruction	0.00%	0.62%	0.36%
loadms w/ 8 regs	0.00%	100.00%	100.00%
mean loadm regs	0	8	8
storems per instruction	0.74%	0.65%	0.69%
storems w/ 5 regs	0.00%	0.13%	0.07%
storems w/ 6 regs	0.00%	0.00%	0.00%
storems w/ 7 regs	100.00%	5.06%	46.89%
storems w/ 8 regs	0.00%	94.81%	53.04%
mean storem regs	7	7.95	7.53
testCompiler			
instructions	33.42%	66.58%	100%
loadms per instruction	0.00%	0.67%	0.45%
loadms w/ 7 regs	0.00%	17.70%	17.70%
loadms w/ 8 regs	0.00%	82.30%	82.30%
mean loadm regs	0	7.82	7.82
storems per instruction	0.75%	0.65%	0.69%
storems w/ 4 regs	0.05%	0.00%	0.02%
storems w/ 5 regs	0.85%	0.12%	0.39%
storems w/ 6 regs	2.72%	0.00%	1.00%
storems w/ 7 regs	96.38%	15.54%	45.21%
storems w/ 8 regs	0.00%	84.33%	53.38%
mean storem regs	6.95	7.84	7.52

Table A.32: Loadm/storem execution frequencies, Part 2.

	ST	SYS	both
testDecompiler			
instructions	32.19%	67.81%	100%
loadms per instruction	0.00%	0.35%	0.24%
loadms w/ 8 regs	0.00%	100.00%	100.00%
mean loadm regs	0	8	8
storems per instruction	0.73%	0.51%	0.58%
storems w/ 4 regs	0.62%	0.00%	0.25%
storems w/ 5 regs	0.00%	0.00%	0.00%
storems w/ 6 regs	0.62%	0.00%	0.25%
storems w/ 7 regs	98.76%	31.02%	58.35%
storems w/ 8 regs	0.00%	68.98%	41.15%
mean storem regs	6.98	7.69	7.40
testPrintDefinition			
instructions	38.01%	61.99%	100%
loadms per instruction	0.00%	0.06%	0.04%
loadms w/ 8 regs	0.00%	100.00%	100.00%
mean loadm regs	0	8.00	8.00
storems per instruction	0.00%	0.14%	0.09%
storems w/ 5 regs	0.00%	2.13%	2.13%
storems w/ 6 regs	0.00%	0.00%	0.00%
storems w/ 7 regs	0.00%	55.32%	55.32%
storems w/ 8 regs	0.00%	42.55%	42.55%
mean storem regs	0	7.38	7.38
testPrintHierarchy			
instructions	26.25%	73.75%	100%
loadms per instruction	0.00%	0.27%	0.20%
loadms w/ 7 regs	0.00%	14.37%	14.37%
loadms w/ 8 regs	0.00%	85.63%	85.63%
mean loadm regs	0	7.86	7.86
storems per instruction	0.24%	0.43%	0.38%
storems w/ 5 regs	0.00%	4.53%	3.79%
storems w/ 6 regs	0.00%	0.00%	0.00%
storems w/ 7 regs	100.00%	41.51%	51.10%
storems w/ 8 regs	0.00%	53.96%	45.11%
mean storem regs	7	7.45	7.38

Table A.32: Loadm/storem execution frequencies, Part 3.			
	ST	SYS	both
	avg of macros		
instructions	34.19%	65.81%	100%
loadms per instruction	0%	0.39%	0.26%
loadms w/ 7 regs	0%	6.41%	6.41%
loadms w/ 8 regs	0%	93.59%	93.59%
mean loadm regs	0	7.94	7.94
storems per instruction	0.49%	0.48%	0.49%
storems w/ 4 regs	0.13%	0%	0.05%
storems w/ 5 regs	0.17%	1.38%	1.28%
storems w/ 6 regs	0.67%	0%	0.25%
storems w/ 7 regs	79.03%	29.69%	51.37%
storems w/ 8 regs	0%	68.93%	47.05%
mean storem regs	5.59	7.66	7.44

Table A.33 shows the performance consequences of eliminated this seldom-used feature. As expected from the frequency data, these instructions have minimal impact. SOAR would be only 3% slower without them.

How much larger would the compiled image grow if we eliminated loadm and storem? Originally, these instructions were intended only for the system code. In that case there would be no significant static impact. However, our current strategy for spill areas requires a routine that allocates a spill area to initialize it. We therefore instrumented our compiler to count the number of words initialized this way (Table A.34). (We also subtracted out the number of retn instructions used solely to write nil into several registers prior to the storem.) Omitting these instructions would increase the size of the system by only 2%.

A.4.4. Performance of Inline Caching

First, we measured the cost of SOAR's in-line cache. In other words, if no procedure lookups were needed, how much faster could SOAR run? To evaluate SOAR's in-line cache, we counted the occurrences of the cache probe conditional trap instruction. That gave us the number of probes. Then, since the prologue takes five cycles, we can easily get the probe time. For the misses, we added two components: the miss trap handler time, obtained by multiplying the number of

Table A.33: Time cost of omitting loadm & storem.
(All costs in percents.)

benchmark	ST	SYS	both
testActivationReturn			
cycles	95.91%	4.09%	100%
loadm cost/all cycles	0%	18.23%	0.75%
storem cost/all cycles	0%	18.23%	0.75%
total cost	0%	36.47%	1.49%
testClassOrganizer			
cycles	42.56%	57.44%	100%
loadm cost	0%	3.11%	1.79%
storem cost	2.99%	3.26%	3.14%
total cost	2.99%	6.37%	4.93%
testCompiler			
cycles	34.07%	65.93%	100%
loadm cost	0%	3.15%	2.08%
storem cost	3.01%	3.08%	3.06%
total cost	3.01%	6.24%	5.14%
testDecompiler			
cycles	32.38%	67.62%	100%
loadm cost	0%	1.71%	1.15%
storem cost	2.98%	2.37%	2.57%
total cost	2.98%	4.07%	3.72%
testPrintDefinition			
cycles	38.09%	61.91%	100%
loadm cost	0%	0.30%	0.19%
storem cost	0%	0.65%	0.40%
total cost	0%	0.96%	0.59%
testPrintHierarchy			
cycles	25.90%	74.10%	100%
loadm cost	0%	1.31%	0.97%
storem cost	1.02%	1.96%	1.72%
total cost	1.02%	3.28%	2.69%
macro avg.			
cycles	34.60%	65.40%	100%
loadm cost	0%	1.92%	1.24%
storem cost	2%	2.26%	2.18%
total cost	2%	4.18%	3.41%

Table A.34: Raw data for static analysis of store multiple.	
description	count
cost for storem	7363 words
total SOAR image size	1500 kB
relative static cost	1.96%

misses (trap instruction traps) by the trap handler path length, and the lookup time, obtained directly from an execution profile. Table A.35 summarizes these data, which show that in-line caching takes a lot of time; 23% of SOAR's time is spent testing the cache and handling misses. Without any caching at all, the probe time would decrease to zero, but the miss time would increase by a factor of 1/3.53%=28. In other words, what takes 100 seconds with in-line caching would take 100–10.88+12.46×28=438 seconds. SOAR would be four times slower with no cache at all.

Next, we compared the 23% cost for the in-line cache with other caching schemes. One of these was the hash table cache found in interpretive Smalltalk-80 systems. The other scheme was an in-line indirect cache. Each call would jump through a per-process area with each process's cache entries. Table A.36 shows the code sequences needed for these two types of cache. The hash table cache is the most expensive scheme, requiring 23 cycles for a cache probe. SOAR's in-line cache requires a prologue of only 5 cycles. The indirect scheme adds a cycle for the indirect call and one for an indirect load in the prologue for a total of 7.

Assuming that the cache miss cost is independent of the caching scheme, we can use the cache probe frequency data to calculate the costs of these caching schemes (Table A.37). The bottom line in the table gives the average speed of the various schemes. SOAR would run only 75% as fast as it does now with a conventional hash table cache. In other words, the work that requires 100 cycles would take 133 with a conventional cache.

Table A.35: Inline cache performance evaluation, Part 1.

description	ST	system	both
testActivationReturn			
instructions	97.21%	2.79%	100%
cycles	95.91%	4.09%	100%
probes per inst	9.47%	0.01%	9.20%
probes per cycle	7.06%	0.01%	6.77%
loadc traps per probe	0%	0%	0%
misses per probe	0%	0%	0%
probe insts per inst	28.40%	0.03%	27.61%
loadc trapH insts per inst	0%	0-0%	0-0%
probe & trapH insts per inst	28.40%	0.03-0.03%	27.61-27.61%
probe cycles per cycle	35.32%	0.03%	33.87%
loadc trapH cycles per cycle	0%	0-0%	0-0%
miss trapH cycles per cycle	0%	0%	0%
probe & trapH cycles per cycle	35.32%	0.03-0.03%	33.87-33.87%
total miss time			0%
total cache time			33.87-33.87%
testClassOrganizer			
instructions	41.06%	58.94%	100%
cycles	42.56%	57.44%	100%
probes per inst	7.24%	0.05%	3.00%
probes per cycle	4.90%	0.04%	2.10%
loadc traps per probe	25.39%	0-0%	25.15-25.15%
misses per probe	0.96%	0%	0.95%
probe insts per inst	21.73%	0.15%	9.01%
loadc trapH insts per inst	5.52%	0-0%	2.27-2.27%
probe & trapH insts per inst	27.24%	0.15-0.15%	11.27-11.27%
probe cycles per cycle	24.48%	0.18%	10.52%
loadc trapH cycles per cycle	8.70%	0-0%	3.70-3.70%
miss trapH cycles per cycle	0.14%	0%	0.06%
probe & trapH cycles per cycle	33.18%	0.18-0.18%	14.22-14.22%
total miss time			2.66%
total cache time			16.88-16.88%

description	ST	system	both
Table A.35: Inline cache performance evaluation, Part 2.			
testCompiler			
instructions	33.42%	66.58%	100%
cycles	34.07%	65.93%	100%
probes per inst	7.29%	0.18%	2.55%
probes per cycle	4.89%	0.12%	1.75%
loadc traps per probe	15.41%	0-1.94%	14.70-14.79%
misses per probe	4.81%	0%	4.59%
probe insts per inst	21.87%	0.53%	7.66%
loadc trapH insts per inst	3.37%	0-0.01%	1.13-1.13%
probe & trapH insts per inst	25.24%	0.53-0.54%	8.79-8.80%
probe cycles per cycle	24.43%	0.61%	8.73%
loadc trapH cycles per cycle	5.27%	0-0.02%	1.80-1.81%
miss trapH cycles per cycle	0.71%	0%	0.24%
probe & trapH cycles per cycle	29.70%	0.61-0.63%	10.52-10.53%
total miss time			15.14%
total cache time			25.66-25.67%
testDecompiler			
instructions	32.19%	67.81%	100%
cycles	32.38%	67.62%	100%
probes per inst	7.20%	0.24%	2.48%
probes per cycle	4.91%	0.16%	1.70%
loadc traps per probe	17.06%	0-0.19%	15.95-15.96%
misses per probe	7.00%	0%	6.54%
probe insts per inst	21.59%	0.72%	7.44%
loadc trapH insts per inst	3.68%	0-0.00%	1.19-1.19%
probe & trapH insts per inst	25.28%	0.72-0.72%	8.62-8.62%
probe cycles per cycle	24.53%	0.82%	8.50%
loadc trapH cycles per cycle	5.86%	0-0.00%	1.90-1.90%
miss trapH cycles per cycle	1.03%	0%	0.33%
probe & trapH cycles per cycle	30.39%	0.82-0.82%	10.40-10.40%
total miss time			24.03%
total cache time			34.43-34.43%

Table A.35: Inline cache performance evaluation, Part 3.

description	ST	system	both
testPrintDefinition			
instructions	38.01%	61.99%	100%
cycles	38.09%	61.91%	100%
probes per inst	7.98%	0.04%	3.06%
probes per cycle	5.83%	0.03%	2.24%
loadc traps per probe	1.03%	0-0%	1.02-1.02%
misses per probe	0.73%	0%	0.72%
probe insts per inst	23.95%	0.12%	9.18%
loadc trapH insts per inst	0.25%	0-0%	0.09-0.09%
probe & trapH insts per inst	24.20%	0.12-0.12%	9.27-9.27%
probe cycles per cycle	29.17%	0.15%	11.21%
loadc trapH cycles per cycle	0.42%	0-0%	0.16-0.16%
miss trapH cycles per cycle	0.13%	0%	0.05%
probe & trapH cycles per cycle	29.59%	0.15-0.15%	11.37-11.37%
total miss time			1.95%
total cache time			13.31-13.31%
testPrintHierarchy			
instructions	26.25%	73.75%	100%
cycles	25.90%	74.10%	100%
probes per inst	7.62%	0.16%	2.12%
probes per cycle	5.44%	0.11%	1.49%
loadc traps per probe	4.47%	0-0%	4.22-4.22%
misses per probe	5.13%	0%	4.84%
probe insts per inst	22.86%	0.48%	6.36%
loadc trapH insts per inst	1.02%	0-0%	0.27-0.27%
probe & trapH insts per inst	23.88%	0.48-0.48%	6.62-6.62%
probe cycles per cycle	27.20%	0.56%	7.46%
loadc trapH cycles per cycle	1.70%	0-0%	0.44-0.44%
miss trapH cycles per cycle	0.84%	0%	0.22%
probe & trapH cycles per cycle	28.90%	0.56-0.56%	7.90-7.90%
total miss time			18.52%
total cache time			26.42-26.42%

Table A.35: Inline cache performance evaluation, Part 4.			
description	ST	system	both
average of macro-benchmarks			
instructions	34.19%	65.81%	100.00%
cycles	34.60%	65.40%	100%
probes per inst	7.47%	0.13%	2.64%
probes per cycle	5.19%	0.09%	1.86%
loadc traps per probe	12.67%	0.00-0.43%	12.21-12.23%
misses per probe	3.73%	0.00%	3.53%
probe insts per inst	22.40%	0.40%	7.93%
loadc trapH insts per inst	2.77%	0.00%	0.99%
probe & trapH insts per inst	25.17%	0.40%	8.91-8.92%
probe cycles per cycle	25.96%	0.46%	9.28%
loadc trapH cycles per cycle	4.39%	0.00%	1.60%
probe & trapH cycles per cycle	30.35%	0.46-0.47%	10.88%
total miss time			12.46%
total cache time			23.34%

Table A.36: Code sequences for various caches.	
Hash-table Cache	
loadc	(r14)classOffset, r6%
%load	(r15)0, r5; sel
%xor	r5, r6, r4%
%load	pcRel(mask), r3%
%and	r3, r4, r4%
%sla	r4, r4%
%sla	r4, r4%
%load	pcRel(base), r3%
%add	r3, r4, r4%
%load	(r4)cacheClass, r3%
%trap3	ne r3, r4%
%load	(r4)cacheSel, r3%
%trap3	ne r3, r4%
%load	(r4)cacheTarget, r3%
%ret	r3, 0%
Time cost: 23 cycles	
Indirect Inline Cache	
<indirect call>	
loadc	(r14)classOffset, r6%
%load	(r15)0, r5%
%load	(r5)rCacheBase, r5; uses global OR mapping
%trap3	ne r5, r6%
Time cost: 7 cycles + 1 cycle for indirect call	
SOAR Inline Cache	
loadc	(r14)classOffset, r6%
%load	(r15)0, r5%
%trap3	ne r5, r6%
Time cost: 5 cycles	

Table A.37: Relative Performance of various caching schemes.					
(SOAR = 100%, faster is better.)					
	no cache	hash table	indirect inline	SOAR cache	zero time resolution
testActivationReturn	151.23%	45.06%	83.04%	100%	151.23%
testClassOrganizer	28.13%	72.53%	91.86%	100%	120.23%
testCompiler	25.05%	76.10%	93.03%	100%	134.11%
testDecompiler	23.35%	76.57%	93.28%	100%	151.74%
testPrintDefinition	28.58%	71.26%	91.67%	100%	115.30%
testPrintHierarchy	22.14%	78.82%	94.19%	100%	135.51%
average	25.45%	75.06%	92.81%	100%	131.38%

Next we examine the space impact of these caching strategies. Table A.38 presents the raw data we have collected from the compiler. The total space taken by SOAR's in-line caching scheme is the sum of the number of extra words needed to hold the last class for the sends (measured by the number of cache slots), and the space consumed by the method prologues. The number of prologues is the same as the number of cache probes. Table A.39 illustrates this prologue. Table A.40 below shows the amounts of overhead at the call site and at the method prologue for the various caching schemes. Finally, we can combine

Table A.38: Raw data for static analysis of caching.	
call sites	22025
cache probes	4654
image size	1500 kB

Table A.39: Inline cache prologue.		
<selector>		needed to handle misses
%loadc	(r14)0, r0	get receiver's class
%load	(r15)0, r1	get last class for send
%trap1	ne r0, r1	verify cache
total length	4 words	

Table A.40: Space overhead for the various caching schemes.		
	call site overhead	prologue overhead
no lookups	0	0
in-line cache	1	4
indirect in-line cache	3	4
hash table	1	0

these data to show the impact that each scheme would have (Table A.41). Thus, the hash table cache would save 1.24% of the image space

A.4.5. How Fast Does SOAR Shuffle?

SOAR is a nimble processor; jumps and branches only take one cycle. To understand the significance of this feature, we can examine the frequency of jumps and calls (Table A.42). As the table shows, jumps and calls are popular instructions; one instruction in 10 is a jump and one in 17 is a call. Given the frequency data, we can add the extra cycle SOAR would require without a fast shuffle (Table A.43). These data show that SOAR would be 11% slower without the fast shuffle mechanism.

A.4.6. Evaluation of Parallel Register Initialization

If the return instruction could write nil into six registers at once, each routine would have to write nil into its temporary variable registers sequentially. Using [Bla83a] page 139, Benchmark column, one can compute an average of

Table A.41: Net space impact of caching schemes.	
no lookups	2.71% savings
in-line cache	0
indirect in-line cache	2.94% cost
hash table	1.24% savings

Table A.42: Frequency of jump and call instructions.

	ST	system	both
testActivationReturn			
instructions	97.21%	2.79%	100%
jumps	5.03%	10.50%	5.18%
calls	9.62%	0.08%	9.35%
jumps & calls	14.65%	10.58%	14.53%
testClassOrganizer			
instructions	41.06%	58.94%	100%
jumps	15.10%	8.96%	11.48%
calls	14.51%	1.14%	6.63%
jumps & calls	29.62%	10.10%	18.11%
testCompiler			
instructions	33.42%	66.58%	100%
jumps	14.25%	8.95%	10.72%
calls	13.74%	1.89%	5.85%
jumps & calls	27.99%	10.84%	16.57%
testDecompiler			
instructions	32.19%	67.81%	100%
jumps	12.91%	8.66%	10.03%
calls	13.23%	1.88%	5.54%
jumps & calls	26.14%	10.55%	15.57%
testPrintDefinition			
instructions	38.01%	61.99%	100%
jumps	12.84%	5.51%	8.30%
calls	13.50%	1.89%	6.30%
jumps & calls	26.34%	7.40%	14.60%
testPrintHierarchy			
instructions	26.25%	73.75%	100%
jumps	12.41%	7.85%	9.04%
calls	13.73%	1.23%	4.51%
jumps & calls	26.14%	9.07%	13.55%
average of macros			
instructions	34.19%	65.81%	100%
jumps	13.50%	7.99%	9.91%
calls	13.74%	1.61%	5.77%
jumps & calls	27.25%	9.59%	15.68%

Table A.43: Cost of omitting fast shuffle.			
	ST	system	both
testActivationReturn			
cycles	95.91%	4.09%	100%
jump cost	3.75%	5.27%	3.82%
call cost	7.17%	0.04%	6.88%
total cost	10.93%	5.31%	10.70%
testClassOrganizer			
cycles	42.56%	57.44%	100%
jump cost	10.21%	6.44%	8.05%
call cost	9.81%	0.82%	4.65%
total cost	20.02%	7.26%	12.69%
testCompiler			
cycles	34.07%	65.93%	100%
jump cost	9.55%	6.18%	7.32%
call cost	9.21%	1.30%	4.00%
total cost	18.76%	7.48%	11.32%
testDecompiler			
cycles	32.38%	67.62%	100%
jump cost	8.80%	5.96%	6.88%
call cost	9.02%	1.30%	3.80%
total cost	17.82%	7.25%	10.67%
testPrintDefinition			
cycles	38.09%	61.91%	100%
jump cost	9.38%	4.04%	6.07%
call cost	9.87%	1.38%	4.61%
total cost	19.25%	5.42%	10.69%
testPrintHierarchy			
cycles	25.90%	74.10%	100%
jump cost	8.86%	5.50%	6.37%
call cost	9.80%	0.86%	3.18%
total cost	18.66%	6.36%	9.55%
average of macro benchmarks			
cycles	34.60%	65.40%	100%
call cost	9.54%	1.13%	4.05%
jump cost	9.36%	5.62%	6.94%
total cost	18.90%	6.75%	10.98%

1.19 arguments and temporaries per call, excluding the receiver. Since the average number of arguments per call is 0.88 [MeC83] (pp 185, Fig. 10.3) we assume that the average number of temporaries per call is between zero and one. This gives the number of extra cycles required per call. To measure the number of calls requiring nilling, we used the number of return instructions that changed the window. This way, we also included returns from interrupts. Table A.44

presents our measurement of the extra time that serial instead of parallel nilling would take, assuming no changes in compiler strategy. The data show that

Table A.44: Evaluation of parallel nilling, Part 1.			
	ST	system	both
testActivationReturn			
instructions	97.21%	2.79%	100%
cycles	95.91%	4.09%	100%
avg. regs containing pointers per retw*	n.a.	2	n.a.
avg temp vars	0-1	n.a.	n.a.
retw'sφa per inst	9.62%	0.06%	9.35%
retw'sφa per cycle	7.17%	0.03%	6.88%
cost of nilling	0%-7.18%	0.06%	0.00%-6.88%
testClassOrganizer			
instructions	41.06%	58.94%	100%
cycles	42.56%	57.44%	100%
avg. regs containing pointers per retw*	n.a.	1.60	n.a.
avg temp vars	0-1	n.a.	n.a.
retw'sφa per inst	9.78%	4.62%	6.74%
retw'sφa per cycle	6.61%	3.32%	4.72%
cost of nilling	0%-6.62%	5.32%	3.05%-5.82%
testCompiler			
instructions	33.42%	66.58%	100%
cycles	34.07%	65.93%	100%
avg. regs containing pointers per retw*	n.a.	1.78	n.a.
avg temp vars	0-1	n.a.	n.a.
retw'sφa per inst	9.64%	3.82%	5.77%
retw'sφa per cycle	6.46%	2.64%	3.94%
cost of nilling	0%-6.46%	4.70%	3.10%-5.30%
testDecompiler			
instructions	32.19%	67.81%	100%
cycles	32.38%	67.62%	100%
avg. regs containing pointers per retw*	n.a.	1.84	n.a.
avg temp vars	0-1	n.a.	n.a.
retw'sφa per inst	8.76%	3.62%	5.27%
retw'sφa per cycle	5.97%	2.49%	3.62%
cost of nilling	0%-5.97%	4.59%	3.10%-5.04%
testPrintDefinition			
instructions	38.01%	61.99%	100%
cycles	38.09%	61.91%	100%
avg. regs containing pointers per retw*	n.a.	1.53	n.a.
avg temp vars	0-1	n.a.	n.a.
retw'sφa per inst	8.19%	5.52%	6.53%
retw'sφa per cycle	5.98%	4.04%	4.78%
cost of nilling	0%-5.99%	6.20%	3.84%-6.12%

Table A.44: Evaluation of parallel nilling, Part 2.			
	ST	system	both
testPrintHierarchy			
instructions	26.25%	73.75%	100%
cycles	25.90%	74.10%	100%
avg. regs containing pointers per retw*	n.a.	2.26	n.a.
avg temp vars	0-1	n.a.	n.a.
retw'sϕa per inst	8.68%	2.79%	4.33%
retw'sϕa per cycle	6.20%	1.95%	3.05%
cost of nilling	0%-6.20%	4.42%	3.28%-4.89%
average of macro-benchmarks			
instructions	34.19%	65.81%	100.00%
cycles	34.60%	65.40%	100.00%
avg. regs containing pointers per retw*	n.a.	1.80	n.a.
avg temp vars	0-1	n.a.	n.a.
retw'sϕa per inst	9.01%	4.07%	5.73%
retw'sϕa per cycle	6.24%	2.89%	4.02%
cost of nilling	0.00%-6.25%	5.05%	3.27%-5.44%

SOAR would run 4% slower without parallel nilling.

To analyze the impact of parallel nilling on the size of the compiled image, we instrumented our compiler (Table A.45). To do this, we kept a running total of the number of temporary variables that would be kept in registers. Assuming that each variable would require an additional instruction to nill it, we can then compute the space overhead nilling would require without hardware support. The table shows that our image would be 1.29% larger if SOAR lacked this feature.

A.4.7. Return Options

The inclusion of three optional operations in SOAR's return instruction add some complexity to the architecture. Which of the possible combinations are really used? Table A.46 shows our dynamic frequency data. As expected, the

---

* includes all return instructions that change register windows: retw, retiw, retnw, retinw — tagged or untagged.

Table A.45: Static analysis of parallel nilling.	
nilling cost for temporary variables	2348
nilling cost for spill initialization	2472
total SOAR image size	1500 kB
relative static cost to nil temps	0.63%
relative static cost to nil spill obj.	0.66%
total static cost for serial nilling	1.29%

Table A.46: Dynamic frequency of return options, Part 1.	
testActivationReturn	
returns per instruction	9.78%
returns per cycle	7.20%
%reti's per return	1.48%
%retn's per return	1.48%
%retnw's per return	0.01%
retnw's per return	95.54%
%retiw's per return	1.48%
testClassOrganizer	
returns per instruction	8.03%
returns per cycle	6.46%
%ret's per return	4.72%
%reti's per return	12.59%
%retn's per return	5.90%
retn's per return	0.03%
%retw's per return	2.26%
retw's per return	0.48%
%retnw's per return	11.92%
retnw's per return	58.20%
%retiw's per return	3.90%
testCompiler	
returns per instruction	8.18%
returns per cycle	5.59%
%ret's per return	3.91%
%reti's per return	11.78%
%retn's per return	9.24%
retn's per return	0.13%
%retw's per return	1.58%
retw's per return	0.53%
%retnw's per return	16.07%
retnw's per return	52.16%
%retiw's per return	4.48%
%retinw's per return	0.12%

Table A.46: Dynamic frequency of return options, Part 2.

testDecompiler	
returns per instruction	7.38%
returns per cycle	5.06%
%ret's per return	4.73%
%reti's per return	11.37%
%retn's per return	8.77%
retn's per return	0.36%
%retw's per return	0.55%
retw's per return	0.02%
%retnw's per return	13.33%
retnw's per return	57.61%
%retiw's per return	3.26%
testPrintDefinition	
returns per instruction	7.84%
returns per cycle	5.74%
%ret's per return	8.45%
%reti's per return	5.87%
%retn's per return	1.90%
%retw's per return	4.74%
%retnw's per return	11.48%
retnw's per return	67.08%
%retiw's per return	0.47%
testPrintHierarchy	
returns per instruction	5.68%
returns per cycle	4.00%
%ret's per return	5.29%
%reti's per return	7.18%
%retn's per return	7.76%
retn's per return	0.17%
%retw's per return	1.02%
%retnw's per return	12.84%
retnw's per return	62.64%
%retiw's per return	3.04%
%retinw's per return	0.06%

Table A.46: Dynamic frequency of return options, Part 3.	
average of macro-benchmarks	
returns per instruction	7.42%
returns per cycle	5.37%
%ret's per return	5.42%
%reti's per return	9.76%
%retn's per return	6.71%
retn's per return	0.14%
%retw's per return	2.03%
retw's per return	0.21%
%retiw's per return	3.03%
%retnw's per return	13.13%
retnw's per return	59.54%
%retinw's per return	0.04%

normal return, *retnw* was used nearly three quarters of the time. Although seven out of the eight possible versions were actually used, only *ret, reti, retw*, and *retnw* are essential, the rest could be omitted. The other 10% of the returns would just require an extra cycle or two to synthesize. Since a return only occurs about one in twenty cycles, the effect would be to add a cycle or two every 200 cycles. This would degrade performance less than 1%.

A.5. Storage Management

This section contains an evaluation of SOAR's features to help manage storage.

A.5.1. Evaluation of the Generation Scavenge Tag Checking Hardware

The first step in understanding the performance impact of eliminating tagged store instructions from SOAR is an execution frequency measurement (Table A.47). At 0.36%, tagged stores are quite rare.

The second step is to examine the cost of doing the check in software (Table A.48): simulating this feature takes four cycles. The number of tagged stores executed per cycle can then be multiplied by the simulation cost (Table A.49). The

Table A.47: Dynamic frequency of tagged store instructions.
(Given as percentage of total instructions executed.)

benchmark	instruction split		tagged store frequency		
	ST	system	ST	system	both
testPopStoreInstVar	81.28%	18.72%	28.47%	0%	23.14%
testClassOrganizer	41.06%	58.94%	0.51%	0.08%	0.26%
testCompiler	33.42%	66.58%	1.20%	0.71%	0.87%
testDecompiler	32.19%	67.81%	0.84%	0.35%	0.51%
testPrintDefinition	38.01%	61.99%	0.18%	0.00%	0.07%
testPrintHierarchy	26.25%	73.75%	0.27%	0.05%	0.11%
avg macros	34.19%	65.81%	0.6%	0.24%	0.36%

Table A.48: Writearound for tagged stores.

%store	(a)i, b
%and	a, 0xf << 28, ta
%and	b, 0xf << 28, tb
%trap	lt ta, tb; trap if a younger
%trap	eq ta, 0xf; trap if a is a context
dynamic cost:	4 cycles
static cost:	4 words

Table A.49: Time cost of omitting GS Tag Trap Store.
(% of total cycles)

benchmark	all cycles		store cost cycles		
	ST	system	ST	system	both
testPopStoreInstVar	83.37%	16.63%	70.59%	0%	58.85%
testClassOrganizer	42.56%	57.44%	1.74%	0.33%	0.93%
testCompiler	34.07%	65.93%	3.99%	2.43%	2.96%
testDecompiler	32.38%	67.62%	2.87%	1.24%	1.76%
testPrintDefinition	38.09%	61.91%	0.66%	0%	0.25%
testPrintHierarchy	25.90%	74.10%	0.93%	0.18%	0.38%
macro avg	34.6%	65.4%	2.04%	0.84%	1.26%

result of this calculation is that the worst-case macro-benchmark would run only 3% slower without this feature.

Next we examine the space cost of eliminating the generation tag checking hardware. Table A.50 gives the static frequency of these store instructions. As expected from the rarity of execution, tagged stores account for very little of the code, or about 2%.

Finally, we multiply the 3 word space penalty by the static frequency (Table A.51) to compute that the Smalltalk-80 image would grow by only 3% if tagged stores were removed from SOAR.

A.5.2. Frequency of GS traps

One last interesting measurement is the cost of the Generation Scavenging trap. Table A.52 gives the frequency of store traps. These data indicate that only 3.9% of the tagged stores trap. Since the path length for the store trap handler is 40 cycles (including the code to *remember* the object), the time spent handling these traps is

$$40 \frac{cycles}{trap} \times 3.9\% \frac{traps}{tagged store} \times 0.36\% \frac{tagged stores}{instruction} \times \frac{1 instruction}{1.5 cycles} = 0.37\%.$$

The time for store traps is insignificant.

Table A.50: Static frequency of tagged stores.		
count of stores	portion of code	portion of code+data
3578	2.12%	0.95%

Table A.51: Space cost of omitting tagged stores.		
count of stores	portion of code	portion of code+data
3578	6.16%	2.85%

Table A.52: Dynamic frequency of tagged store GS traps.			
(Given as percentage of ST, system, both tagged stores executed.)			
benchmark	ST	system	both
testPopStoreInstVar	0%	0%	0%
testClassOrganizer	0.30%	0%	0.24%
testCompiler	0.24%	4.83%	2.71%
testDecompiler	0%	0%	0%
testPrintDefinition	2.63%	0%	2.63%
testPrintHierarchy	21.05%	0%	13.79%
avg macros	4.84%	0.97%	3.87%

A.5.3. Evaluating the Pointer to Register Support

The pointer-to-register circuitry includes a comparator and a significant amount of control complexity [Pen85b]. How well could SOAR get along without it? There are two cases to analyze:

thisContext

In Smalltalk-80, a routine can request a pointer to its activation record by accessing the pseudo-variable *thisContext*. In this case, the compiler must give out an illegal (unmapped) address. When the program tries to use this address, the page fault handler can then ensure the activation record resides in memory and not on-chip, then complete the operation. Fortunately, this case mostly occurs in the debugger, where a speed penalty is more acceptable.

blockCopy

A Smalltalk-80 *block* permits execution of a piece of code in one procedure to be controlled by another procedure. We implement this feature with a distinct activation record that contains a pointer to the defining activation record. Thus, the code in a *block* can access the data in its home activation record with loads and stores. If we eliminate the pointer-to-register circuitry from SOAR, we merely need to flush a block's home activation record out to memory when entering the block. This may involve flushing extra register windows until we reach the desired one. On the other hand, the desired window may already be in memory. We ran the benchmarks and simulated the cost of this scheme. Every time control entered a *block*, we counted the number of windows that would have to be flushed. The first column of Table A.53 give the number of block invocations, and the second gives the average number of windows flushed per invocation. We have assumed an 18 cycle cost to flush a window; nine cycles to save it, and another nine to restore it. This estimate is probably low since it omits the cost of handling the extra traps. The third column, which is the cycles spent flushing windows per invocation, is just 18 times the second. The next two columns give the frequency of block invocations per cycle in compiled Smalltalk code, and the cost of simulating pointer-to-register per cycle in compiled Smalltalk code. Finally, the last two columns give the same data, but relative to the total time, not just the time executing compiled code. These data show that SOAR would be only 3% slower without the pointer-to-register feature.

Table A.53: Time cost of eliminating pointer-to-register hardware.						
benchmark	block invoks	windows/ invok	cycles/ invok	values/ ST cycle	cost/ ST cycle	values/ cycle	cost/ cycle
classOrganizer	4023	0.92	16.6	0.29%	4.89%	0.13%	2.08%
compiler	906	0.50	9.0	0.24%	2.20%	0.08%	0.75%
decompiler	2785	1.40	25.2	0.30%	7.49%	0.10%	2.43%
printDefinition	149	2.02	36.4	0.53%	19.2%	0.20%	7.31%
printHierarchy	152	1.30	23.4	0.50%	11.68%	0.13%	3.02%
average	1603	1.23	22.1	0.37%	9.09%	0.13%	3.12%

A.6. Implementation

We have examined two implementation-related issues: eliminating register forwarding and the relative proportions of data- and instruction-fetches.

A.6.1. Register Forwarding

How important is the register forwarding in SOAR's datapath? To get a crude idea, we measured how often our simulated instructions used a forwarded value and assessed a penalty of one cycle. Table A.54 shows the results of this measurement. Forwarding is important; SOAR would run 15% slower without it. It is possible though, that there might be a way to approach the speed of automatic forwarding without the complexity of detecting forwarding at runtime.

Table A.54: Time cost for eliminating forwarding.			
testClassOrganizer			
cycles	42.56%	57.44%	100%
extra time for pipeline bubbles	9.72%	14.02%	12.19%
testCompiler			
cycles	34.07%	65.93%	100%
extra time for pipeline bubbles	10.26%	14.67%	13.17%
testDecompiler			
cycles	32.38%	67.62%	100%
extra time for pipeline bubbles	10.66%	16.88%	14.86%
testPrintDefinition			
cycles	38.09%	61.91%	100%
extra time for pipeline bubbles	9.81%	21.31%	16.93%
testPrintHierarchy			
cycles	25.90%	74.10%	100%
extra time for pipeline bubbles	10.39%	21.22%	18.41%
average of macro-benchmarks			
cycles	34.60%	65.40%	100.00%
extra time for pipeline bubbles	10.17%	17.62%	15.11%

Two interesting approaches are special instruction scheduling or access to the forwarded value in a special register [Pen85b]. (See Section 2.5.3: MIPS.)

A.6.2. Memory Accesses

In this section, we examine the proportion of memory references for instructions and data. There are three different types of SOAR memory references:

I-fetches

These are normal instruction fetches, derived from the simulator's instruction count.

D-fetches

These are data references, computed from the number of load, store, loadc, loadm, and storem instructions. (We weighted each loadm and storem by the number of words accessed.)

I-flushes

I-flushes represent instructions fetched but not executed. Examples include skipped instructions and instructions after returns. These are the cycles left over when the above two are subtracted from the total number of cycles.

Table A.55 presents our analysis. The rarity of I-flushes, 9%, supports our suspicion that keeping SOAR's pipeline short keeps its utilization high.

Table A.55: Instruction vs. Data Fetches, Part 1.			
	ST	system	both
test3plus4			
all instruction references	65.14%	34.86%	100%
all data references	32.08%	67.92%	100%
all data + instruction references	61.15%	38.85%	100%
I-fetches per cycle	90.73%	71.56%	82.98%
I-flushes per cycle	3.15%	9.33%	5.65%
D-fetches per cycle	6.12%	19.11%	11.37%
testActivationReturn			
all instruction references	97.21%	2.79%	100%
all data references	88.17%	11.83%	100%
all data + instruction references	95.65%	4.35%	100%
I-fetches per cycle	74.61%	50.20%	73.61%
I-flushes per cycle	11.26%	5.32%	11.02%
D-fetches per cycle	14.13%	44.48%	15.37%
testClassOrganizer			
all instruction references	41.06%	58.94%	100%
all data references	40.60%	59.40%	100%
all data + instruction references	40.97%	59.03%	100%
I-fetches per cycle	79.74%	80.80%	80.37%
I-flushes per cycle	1.44%	0%*	0.46%
D-fetches per cycle	18.82%	19.43%	19.18%
testCompiler			
all instruction references	33.42%	66.58%	100%
all data references	33.88%	66.12%	100%
all data + instruction references	33.53%	66.47%	100%
I-fetches per cycle	67.02%	68.98%	68.31%
I-flushes per cycle	13.31%	11.19%	11.91%
D-fetches per cycle	19.67%	19.83%	19.78%

---

* Our simulator computed a value of -0.24% for this entry, clear evidence that our instruction counts are inexact.

Table A.55: Instruction vs. Data Fetches, Part 2.			
	ST	system	both
testDecompiler			
all instruction references	32.19%	67.81%	100%
all data references	33.27%	66.73%	100%
all data + instruction references	32.42%	67.58%	100%
I-fetches per cycle	68.17%	68.76%	68.57%
I-flushes per cycle	12.57%	12.75%	12.69%
D-fetches per cycle	19.26%	18.50%	18.74%
testPrintDefinition			
all instruction references	38.01%	61.99%	100%
all data references	36.82%	63.18%	100%
all data + instruction references	37.78%	62.22%	100%
I-fetches per cycle	73.08%	73.33%	73.23%
I-flushes per cycle	10.32%	9.14%	9.59%
D-fetches per cycle	16.61%	17.53%	17.18%
testPrintHierarchy			
all instruction references	26.25%	73.75%	100%
all data references	23.28%	76.72%	100%
all data + instruction references	25.62%	74.38%	100%
I-fetches per cycle	71.39%	70.11%	70.44%
I-flushes per cycle	11.66%	10.36%	10.70%
D-fetches per cycle	16.95%	19.53%	18.86%
average of macro-benchmarks			
all instruction references	34.19%	65.81%	100.00%
all data references	33.57%	66.43%	100.00%
all data + instruction references	34.06%	65.94%	100.00%
I-fetches per cycle	71.88%	72.40%	72.18%
I-flushes per cycle	9.86%	8.64%	9.07%
D-fetches per cycle	18.26%	18.96%	18.75%

Appendix B

Raw SOAR Data

B.1. Introduction

This appendix contains the raw data we gathered and used for the calculations in Appendix A. The first section contains instruction mixes for the second iteration of several benchmarks. These were run in an image that was modified to eliminate almost all occurrences of the become primitive, as outlined in Chapter 5. The second section contains execution time profiles for the same runs. To guide the reader through this section, we have reprinted part of the table of contents in Table B.1.

Table B.1: Table of contents for Appendix B.

B.2. Instruction Mix Data

This section contains our instruction mix data. A few definitions are in order:

- *steps:* the number of instructions executed.

- *cycles:* the number of SOAR cycles executed. This is a measure of execution time.

- *ST:* the code that was written in Smalltalk and compiled.

- *system:* the runtime system support primitives written in assembler language.

- *Ccodes:* simulator operations, mostly print statements used for tracing.

- *TI:* trap instruction traps.

- *TT:* tag traps.

- *GS:* Generation Scavenging traps.

- *WO:* register window overflow traps.

- *WU:* register window underflow traps. *TT:* tag traps.

- *loadm/storem [1-8]:* the number of loadm or storem instructions that accessed a given number of registers.

- *ret*w's:* return instructions of any type that changed windows.

- *nonNil8-14:* At every ret*w, the simulator counts the number of registers between r8 and r14 that contain something other than nil. This figure is the total for the run.

- *int8-14:* the accumulated total of registers between r8 and r14 that contain integers when a ret*w is executed.

- *taggedImm:* the immediate value could not have been represented without SOAR's tagged immediate feature.

- *untaggedImm:* the immediate value could have been represented without SOAR's tagged immediate feature.
- *condJumps:* the number of times a jump immediately followed a skip.

Table B.2: test3plus4 Micro-Benchmark Instruction Mix.			
	ST	system	both
Steps			4642
Cycles	3332	2261	5593
Ccodes	3	0	3
%nop	1	0	1
%ret	0	100	100
%retn	1	0	1
%retnw	100	3	103
retnw	1	102	103
%skip	0	115	115
trap1	0	100	100
%trap3	101	1	102
%store	0	20	20
%load	103	411	514
loadc	101	1	102
%and	0	4	4
%or	0	3	3
%add	1406	429	1835
add	1000	0	1000
%sub	0	107	107
%extract	0	1	1
%insert	0	3	3
			0
%jump	102	107	209
jump	2	4	6
%call	0	4	4
call	102	103	205

Table B.3: testPopStoreInstanceVar. Micro-Benchmark Inst. Mix.			
	ST	system	both
Steps			8642
Cycles	11332	2261	13593
Ccodes	3	0	3
%nop	1	0	1
%ret	0	100	100
%retn	1	0	1
%retnw	100	3	103
retnw	1	102	103
%skip	0	115	115

Table B.3: testPopStoreInstanceVar. Micro-Benchmark Inst. Mix.

	ST	system	both
trap1	0	100	100
%trap3	101	1	102
%store	0	20	20
store	2000	0	2000
%load	2103	411	2514
loadc	101	1	102
%and	0	4	4
%or	0	3	3
%add	2406	429	2835
%sub	0	107	107
%extract	0	1	1
%insert	0	3	3
%jump	102	107	209
jump	2	4	6
%call	0	4	4
call	102	103	205

Table B.4: testActivationReturn Micro-Benchmark Instruction Mix.

	ST	system	both
Steps			356067
Cycles	463922	19772	483694
WO	515	0	515
WU	513	2	515
Ccodes	3	0	3
%nop	1	515	516
%ret	0	1	1
%retn	1	515	516
%retnw	2	3	5
retnw	33280	5	33285
%reti	0	515	515
%retiw	0	515	515
%skip	0	1049	1049
skip	32767	0	32767
trap1	0	1	1
%trap2	16383	0	16383
%trap3	32769	1	32770
%store	0	20	20
%storem	0	515	515
%load	32771	534	33305
loadc	32769	1	32770
%loadm	0	515	515
%and	0	4	4

Table B.4: testActivationReturn Micro-Benchmark Instruction Mix.

	ST	system	both
%or	0	3	3
%add	81926	2607	84533
%sub	0	1552	1552
sub	32766	0	32766
%extract	0	1	1
%insert	0	3	3
%jump	1033	523	1556
jump	16385	519	16904
%call	0	4	4
call	33285	4	33289
WO 0?	515	0	515
WU retnw	513	2	515
loadm 8	0	515	515
storem 8	0	515	515
ret*w's	33284	6	33290
nonNil8-14	99341	25	99366
int8-14	33285	13	33298
eq %skip	0	528	528
eq skip	32767	0	32767
ne %skip	0	518	518
ne trap1	0	1	1
ne %trap3	32769	1	32770
ltu/in0 %skip	0	1	1
geu/out0 %trap2	16383	0	16383
leu %skip	0	1	1
gtu %skip	0	1	1
untaggedImm %ret	0	1	1
untaggedImm %retn	1	515	516
untaggedImm %retnw	1	3	4
untaggedImm retnw	32768	3	32771
untaggedImm %reti	0	515	515
untaggedImm %retiw	0	515	515
untaggedImm %skip	0	518	518
untaggedImm skip	32767	0	32767
untaggedImm %load	32770	12	32782
untaggedImm loadc	32769	1	32770
untaggedImm %loadm	0	515	515
untaggedImm %and	0	2	2
untaggedImm %add	7	2081	2088
untaggedImm %sub	0	1551	1551
untaggedImm sub	32766	0	32766
untaggedImm %extract	0	1	1

Table B.4: testActivationReturn Micro-Benchmark Instruction Mix.

	ST	system	both
untaggedImm %insert	0	3	3
taggedImm %skip	0	1	1
taggedImm %trap2	16383	0	16383
taggedImm %load	1	522	523
taggedImm %and	0	1	1
taggedImm %or	0	2	2
taggedImm %add	0	519	519

Table B.5: testClassOrganizer Macro-Benchmark Instruction Mix.

	ST	system	both
Steps			1953882
Cycles	1156735	1638604	2795339
Ccodes	1482	0	1482
TT	15025	0	15025
WO	6088	949	7037
WU	4692	2345	7037
TI	641	9	650
GS	25	0	25
%nop	1	9857	9858
%ret	5	8516	8521
%retw	0	4073	4073
retw	0	870	870
%retn	2051	8599	10650
retn	0	47	47
%retnw	7429	14080	21509
retnw	19660	85371	105031
%reti	0	22728	22728
%retiw	0	7037	7037
%retinw	0	9	9
%skip	11154	136263	147417
skip	18607	11737	30344
%trap1	0	12466	12466
trap1	0	31372	31372
%trap2	13507	412	13919
%trap3	57631	653	58284
%trap4	1318	12	1330
%store	9821	23075	32896
store	4697	1177	5874
%storem	5320	7483	12803
%load	108290	160134	268424
load	0	17044	17044
loadc	57631	1326	58957
%loadm	0	7037	7037
%srl	0	43097	43097

Table B.5: testClassOrganizer Macro-Benchmark Instruction Mix.

	ST	system	both
%xor	0	12044	12044
%and	5	36562	36567
%or	1318	9919	11237
%add	218244	229098	447342
add	10076	12235	22311
%sll	0	18023	18023
sll	0	5756	5756
%sub	1318	41742	43060
sub	2357	21503	23860
%extract	0	44618	44618
%insert	0	12721	12721
%jump	85710	34846	120556
jump	31288	62388	93676
%call	0	8578	8578
call	114110	6343	120453
TT skip	3893	0	3893
TT loadc	11132	0	11132
WO 0?	6088	949	7037
WU retw	0	489	489
WU retnw	4692	1856	6548
TI trap1	0	9	9
TI trap3	641	0	641
GS retnw	11	0	11
GS store	14	0	14
loadm 8	0	7037	7037
storem 5	0	11	11
storem 7	5320	435	5755
storem 8	0	7037	7037
ret*w's	75521	55960	131481
nonNil8-14	192227	224667	416894
int8-14	68182	131169	199351
always %skip	3404	3	3407
lt %skip	0	8671	8671
lt skip	276	5123	5399
ge %skip	0	8526	8526
ge skip	14	144	158
ge trap1	0	262	262
eq %skip	7179	36799	43978
eq skip	6013	442	6455
eq %trap1	0	190	190
eq trap1	0	1461	1461
eq %trap4	1318	12	1330

Table B.5: testClassOrganizer Macro-Benchmark Instruction Mix.

	ST	system	both
ne %skip	571	58466	59037
ne %trap1	0	7612	7612
ne trap1	0	3982	3982
ne %trap3	57631	653	58284
le %skip	0	17063	17063
le skip	7952	242	8194
gt %skip	0	101	101
gt skip	459	5786	6245
gt %trap1	0	136	136
gt trap1	0	131	131
ltu/in0 %skip	0	747	747
geu/out0 %skip	0	3928	3928
geu/out0 %trap1	0	4528	4528
geu/out0 trap1	0	25536	25536
geu/out0 %trap2	13507	412	13919
leu %skip	0	1168	1168
gtu %skip	0	791	791
untaggedImm %ret	0	4623	4623
untaggedImm %retw	0	39	39
untaggedImm retw	0	522	522
untaggedImm %retn	2051	8599	10650
untaggedImm retn	0	47	47
untaggedImm %retnw	6180	13938	20118
untaggedImm retnw	16217	83657	99874
untaggedImm %reti	0	22728	22728
untaggedImm %retiw	0	7037	7037
untaggedImm %retinw	0	9	9
untaggedImm %skip	0	26794	26794
untaggedImm skip	4916	87	5003
untaggedImm %trap1	0	144	144
untaggedImm %load	102730	90070	192800
untaggedImm load	0	17044	17044
untaggedImm loadc	57631	1326	58957
untaggedImm %loadm	0	7037	7037
untaggedImm %xor	0	3015	3015
untaggedImm %and	0	29187	29187
untaggedImm %or	0	5	5
untaggedImm %add	20011	152781	172792
untaggedImm add	9405	22	9427
untaggedImm %sub	1318	35799	37117
untaggedImm sub	669	16489	17158
untaggedImm %extract	0	26380	26380
untaggedImm %insert	0	2199	2199
taggedImm %skip	3857	21610	25467

Table B.5: testClassOrganizer Macro-Benchmark Instruction Mix.

	ST	system	both
taggedImm %trap1	0	4528	4528
taggedImm %trap2	13507	412	13919
taggedImm %trap4	1318	12	1330
taggedImm %load	5560	42117	47677
taggedImm %and	5	2130	2135
taggedImm %or	1318	1680	2998
taggedImm %add	8955	18331	27286
srl barrel shifter savings	0	12612	12612
forwarding cost	111047	250701	361748
two-tone savings	209716	308810	518526
condJumps	9821	72666	82487

Table B.6: testCompiler Macro-Benchmark Instruction Mix.

	ST	system	both
Steps			743753
Cycles	370941	717817	1088758
Ccodes	1557	0	1557
TT	3372	18	3390
WO	2088	641	2729
WU	1889	840	2729
TI	872	75	947
GS	11	168	179
	0	1	1
%nop	1	13688	13689
%ret	10	2368	2378
%retw	0	960	960
retw	0	320	320
%retn	1212	4410	5622
retn	0	81	81
%retnw	2422	7362	9784
retnw	8528	23221	31749
%reti	0	7170	7170
%retiw	0	2729	2729
%retinw	0	75	75
%skip	3737	77074	80811
skip	4810	4342	9152
%trap1	0	2763	2763
trap1	0	7701	7701
%trap2	4735	259	4994
%trap3	18122	878	19000
%trap4	450	19	469
%store	1880	16253	18133
store	2973	3476	6449
%storem	1876	3236	5112

Table B.6: testCompiler Macro-Benchmark Instruction Mix.

	ST	system	both
%load	36937	65008	101945
load	0	5087	5087
loadc	18121	1235	19356
%loadm	0	3316	3316
%srl	0	9388	9388
%sra	0	50	50
sra	0	24	24
%xor	0	1304	1304
%and	11	13067	13078
and	30	4	34
%or	451	4818	5269
%add	66485	106045	172530
add	3094	4385	7479
%sll	0	5159	5159
sll	0	1406	1406
%sub	450	20291	20741
sub	1124	5830	6954
%extract	0	12979	12979
%insert	0	3697	3697
%jump	26002	24280	50282
jump	9420	20049	29469
%call	0	6801	6801
call	34157	2548	36705
TT skip	579	1	580
TT loadc	2793	17	2810
WO 0?	2088	641	2729
WU retw	0	146	146
WU retnw	1889	694	2583
TI trap1	0	75	75
TI trap3	872	0	872
GS retnw	4	0	4
GS store	7	168	175
loadm 7	0	587	587
loadm 8	0	2729	2729
storem 4	1	0	1
storem 5	16	4	20
storem 6	51	0	51
storem 7	1808	503	2311
storem 8	0	2729	2729
ret*w's	23962	18922	42884
nonNil8-14	62890	80599	143489
int8-14	23225	46848	70073

Table B.6: testCompiler Macro-Benchmark Instruction Mix.			
	ST	system	both
always %skip	944	1	945
lt %skip	0	11216	11216
lt skip	304	1101	1405
ge %skip	0	2640	2640
ge skip	187	102	289
ge trap1	0	110	110
eq %skip	2715	17376	20091
eq skip	1528	1285	2813
eq %trap1	0	190	190
eq trap1	0	358	358
eq %trap4	450	19	469
ne %skip	78	35782	35860
ne skip	2	254	256
ne %trap1	0	1556	1556
ne trap1	0	906	906
ne %trap3	18122	878	19000
le %skip	0	5343	5343
le skip	1469	76	1545
gt %skip	0	68	68
gt skip	741	1523	2264
gt %trap1	0	65	65
gt trap1	0	55	55
ltu/in0 %skip	0	905	905
geu/out0 %skip	0	1818	1818
geu/out0 %trap1	0	952	952
geu/out0 trap1	0	6261	6261
geu/out0 %trap2	4735	259	4994
leu %skip	0	1077	1077
gtu %skip	0	848	848
out1 trap1	0	11	11
untaggedImm %ret	0	1788	1788
untaggedImm %retw	0	360	360
untaggedImm retw	0	194	194
untaggedImm %retn	1212	4410	5622
untaggedImm retn	0	81	81
untaggedImm %retnw	2116	7324	9440
untaggedImm retnw	6945	22565	29510
untaggedImm %reti	0	7170	7170
untaggedImm %retiw	0	2729	2729
untaggedImm %retinw	0	75	75
untaggedImm %skip	0	9993	9993
untaggedImm skip	1658	485	2143
untaggedImm %trap1	0	74	74
untaggedImm %load	33942	47159	81101

Table B.6: testCompiler Macro-Benchmark Instruction Mix.

	ST	system	both
untaggedImm load	0	5087	5087
untaggedImm loadc	18121	1235	19356
untaggedImm %loadm	0	3316	3316
untaggedImm %xor	0	447	447
untaggedImm %and	0	6924	6924
untaggedImm and	17	4	21
untaggedImm %or	1	147	148
untaggedImm %add	8059	70090	78149
untaggedImm add	2189	120	2309
untaggedImm %sub	450	17456	17906
untaggedImm sub	542	4359	4901
untaggedImm %extract	0	10833	10833
untaggedImm %insert	0	2423	2423
taggedImm %skip	1058	17170	18228
taggedImm %trap1	0	952	952
taggedImm %trap2	4735	259	4994
taggedImm %trap4	450	19	469
taggedImm %load	2995	11425	14420
taggedImm %and	11	2306	2317
taggedImm %or	450	1995	2445
taggedImm %add	3662	8732	12394
sll barrel shifter savings	0	3	3
srl barrel shifter savings	0	1900	1900
sra barrel shifter savings	0	24	24
forwarding cost	38049	105324	143373
two-tone savings	68706	91028	159734
condJumps	3416	28601	32017

Table B.7: testDecompiler Macro-Benchmark Instruction Mix.

	ST	system	both
Steps			1983995
Cycles	936933	1956663	2893596
Ccodes	6016	0	6016
TT	8641	6	8647
WO	3225	1548	4773
WU	3433	1340	4773
TI	3217	6	3223
%nop	1	6185	6186
%ret	31	6890	6921
%retw	0	798	798
retw	0	25	25
%retn	4049	8783	12832
retn	0	534	534
%retnw	3975	15526	19501

Table B.7: testDecompiler Macro-Benchmark Instruction Mix.

	ST	system	both
retnw	21194	63099	84293
%reti	0	16637	16637
%retiw	0	4773	4773
%retinw	0	6	6
%skip	4601	236206	240807
skip	15999	8356	24355
%trap1	0	8682	8682
trap1	0	21010	21010
%trap2	12417	788	13205
%trap3	45968	3212	49180
%trap4	1088	82	1170
%store	7926	50609	58535
store	5375	4826	10201
%storem	4680	6919	11599
%load	88555	196228	284783
load	0	14998	14998
loadc	45962	3836	49798
%loadm	0	4773	4773
%srl	0	17159	17159
sra	0	2120	2120
%xor	0	6329	6329
%and	31	36239	36270
and	500	0	500
%or	1088	10335	11423
%add	186538	309908	496446
add	11775	13398	25173
%sll	0	7956	7956
sll	0	1306	1306
%sub	1088	46940	48028
sub	2890	15654	18544
%extract	0	37296	37296
%insert	0	15013	15013
%jump	60263	64066	124329
jump	22167	52476	74643
%call	0	17876	17876
call	84494	7471	91965
TT skip	798	0	798
TT loadc	7843	6	7849
WO 0?	3225	1548	4773
WU retw	0	1	1
WU retnw	3433	1339	4772
TI trap1	0	6	6
TI trap3	3217	0	3217

Table B.7: testDecompiler Macro-Benchmark Instruction Mix.			
	ST	system	both
loadm 8	0	4773	4773
storem 4	29	0	29
storem 6	29	0	29
storem 7	4622	2146	6768
storem 8	0	4773	4773
ret*w's	55944	48679	104623
nonNil8-14	155632	215034	370666
int8-14	56499	125311	181810
always %skip	1726	61	1787
lt %skip	0	44547	44547
lt skip	797	1852	2649
ge %skip	0	4500	4500
ge skip	1095	135	1230
ge trap1	0	168	168
eq %skip	2683	40869	43552
eq skip	5332	734	6066
eq %trap1	0	1022	1022
eq trap1	0	921	921
eq %trap4	1088	82	1170
ne %skip	192	123615	123807
ne skip	0	88	88
ne %trap1	0	5499	5499
ne trap1	0	2875	2875
ne %trap3	45968	3212	49180
le %skip	0	10193	10193
le skip	6112	142	6254
gt skip	1865	5405	7270
gt %trap1	0	115	115
gt trap1	0	84	84
ltu/in0 %skip	0	2961	2961
geu/out0 %skip	0	1015	1015
geu/out0 %trap1	0	2046	2046
geu/out0 trap1	0	16384	16384
geu/out0 %trap2	12417	788	13205
leu %skip	0	5107	5107
gtu %skip	0	3338	3338
out1 trap1	0	578	578
untaggedImm %ret	0	6092	6092
untaggedImm retw	0	24	24
untaggedImm %retn	4049	8783	12832
untaggedImm retn	0	534	534
untaggedImm %retnw	3521	15496	19017
untaggedImm retnw	18215	61790	80005

Table B.7: testDecompiler Macro-Benchmark Instruction Mix.

	ST	system	both
untaggedImm %reti	0	16637	16637
untaggedImm %retiw	0	4773	4773
untaggedImm %retinw	0	6	6
untaggedImm %skip	0	28251	28251
untaggedImm skip	6564	0	6564
untaggedImm %trap1	0	379	379
untaggedImm %load	82930	153764	236694
untaggedImm load	0	14998	14998
untaggedImm loadc	45962	3836	49798
untaggedImm %loadm	0	4773	4773
untaggedImm %xor	0	2070	2070
untaggedImm %and	0	14346	14346
untaggedImm and	267	0	267
untaggedImm %or	0	31	31
untaggedImm %add	24298	199945	224243
untaggedImm add	8025	2309	10334
untaggedImm %sub	1088	40446	41534
untaggedImm sub	1370	12298	13668
untaggedImm %extract	0	30917	30917
untaggedImm %insert	0	8883	8883
taggedImm %skip	1333	61155	62488
taggedImm %trap1	0	2046	2046
taggedImm %trap2	12417	788	13205
taggedImm %trap4	1088	82	1170
taggedImm %load	5625	28232	33857
taggedImm %and	31	6249	6280
taggedImm %or	1088	5019	6107
taggedImm %add	7078	23687	30765
srl barrel shifter savings	0	4473	4473
forwarding cost	99921	330197	430118
two-tone savings	186209	233311	419520
condJumps	8268	62319	70587

Table B.8: testPrintDefinition Macro-Benchmark Instruction Mix.

	ST	system	both
Steps			54310
Cycles	28249	45910	74159
Ccodes	77	0	77
TT	216	0	216
WO	11	9	20
WU	13	7	20
TI	12	0	12
GS	2	0	2
%nop	1	23	24

Table B.8: testPrintDefinition Macro-Benchmark Instruction Mix.			
	ST	system	both
%ret	0	360	360
%retw	0	202	202
%retn	38	43	81
%retnw	165	324	489
retnw	368	2489	2857
%reti	0	250	250
%retiw	0	20	20
%skip	284	3116	3400
skip	891	5	896
%trap1	0	644	644
trap1	0	1238	1238
%trap2	282	2	284
%trap3	1648	14	1662
%store	148	1066	1214
store	38	0	38
%storem	0	47	47
%load	2857	5571	8428
load	0	866	866
loadc	1648	38	1686
%loadm	0	20	20
%srl	0	868	868
%xor	0	621	621
%and	0	1238	1238
and	1	0	1
%or	0	292	292
%add	6277	6745	13022
add	469	460	929
%sll	0	199	199
%sub	0	726	726
sub	14	908	922
%extract	0	2031	2031
%insert	0	750	750
%jump	1650	923	2573
jump	1000	932	1932
%call	0	362	362
call	2787	273	3060
TT skip	199	0	199
TT loadc	17	0	17
WO 0?	11	9	20
WU retnw	13	7	20
TI trap3	12	0	12
GS retnw	1	0	1
GS store	1	0	1

Table B.8: testPrintDefinition Macro-Benchmark Instruction Mix.

	ST	system	both
loadm 8	0	20	20
storem 5	0	1	1
storem 7	0	26	26
storem 8	0	20	20
ret*w's	1690	1857	3547
nonNil8-14	4554	7923	12477
int8-14	1387	5077	6464
always %skip	11	0	11
lt %skip	0	58	58
ge skip	0	4	4
ge trap1	0	4	4
eq %skip	273	1379	1652
eq skip	17	0	17
eq %trap1	0	12	12
ne %skip	0	1107	1107
ne skip	0	1	1
ne %trap1	0	428	428
ne trap1	0	149	149
ne %trap3	1648	14	1662
le %skip	0	227	227
le skip	417	0	417
gt %skip	0	1	1
gt skip	258	0	258
gt %trap1	0	2	2
gt trap1	0	2	2
ltu/in0 %skip	0	39	39
geu/out0 %skip	0	199	199
geu/out0 %trap1	0	202	202
geu/out0 trap1	0	1083	1083
geu/out0 %trap2	282	2	284
leu %skip	0	64	64
gtu %skip	0	42	42
untaggedImm %ret	0	161	161
untaggedImm %retw	0	3	3
untaggedImm %retn	38	43	81
untaggedImm %retnw	160	324	484
untaggedImm retnw	360	2482	2842
untaggedImm %reti	0	250	250
untaggedImm %retiw	0	20	20
untaggedImm %skip	0	992	992
untaggedImm skip	26	0	26
untaggedImm %trap1	0	4	4
untaggedImm %load	2725	3667	6392

Table B.8: testPrintDefinition Macro-Benchmark Instruction Mix.

	ST	system	both
untaggedImm load	0	866	866
untaggedImm loadc	1648	38	1686
untaggedImm %loadm	0	20	20
untaggedImm %xor	0	217	217
untaggedImm %and	0	910	910
untaggedImm %add	329	4601	4930
untaggedImm add	469	0	469
untaggedImm %sub	0	693	693
untaggedImm sub	8	679	687
untaggedImm %extract	0	1423	1423
untaggedImm %insert	0	114	114
taggedImm %skip	7	531	538
taggedImm %trap1	0	202	202
taggedImm %trap2	282	2	284
taggedImm %load	132	972	1104
taggedImm %and	0	55	55
taggedImm %or	0	53	53
taggedImm %add	412	193	605
srl barrel shifter savings	0	434	434
forwarding cost	2770	9784	12554
two-tone savings	5800	9344	15144
condJumps	299	1281	1580

Table B.9: testPrintHierarchy Macro-Benchmark Instruction Mix.

	ST	system	both
Steps			82833
Cycles	30458	87127	117585
Ccodes	193	0	193
TT	86	0	86
WO	117	26	143
WU	81	62	143
TI	85	3	88
GS	24	0	24
%nop	1	169	170
%ret	0	249	249
%retw	0	48	48
%retn	109	256	365
retn	0	8	8
%retnw	208	396	604
retnw	618	2329	2947
%reti	0	338	338
%retiw	0	143	143
%retinw	0	3	3
%skip	261	8996	9257

Table B.9: testPrintHierarchy Macro-Benchmark Instruction Mix.			
	ST	system	both
skip	545	35	580
%trap1	0	1148	1148
trap1	0	1324	1324
%trap2	303	6	309
%trap3	1657	98	1755
%trap4	13	0	13
%store	176	2595	2771
store	57	30	87
%storem	52	265	317
%load	2908	10094	13002
load	0	890	890
loadc	1657	117	1774
%loadm	0	167	167
%srl	0	1308	1308
%xor	0	1782	1782
%and	0	1955	1955
and	4	0	4
%or	13	643	656
%add	6770	12942	19712
add	452	155	607
%sll	0	22	22
sll	0	3	3
%sub	13	2218	2231
sub	50	513	563
%extract	0	2567	2567
%insert	0	1734	1734
%jump	1870	2509	4379
jump	828	2284	3112
%call	0	547	547
call	2986	202	3188
TT skip	12	0	12
TT loadc	74	0	74
WO 0?	117	26	143
WU retnw	81	62	143
TI trap1	0	3	3
TI trap3	85	0	85
GS retnw	12	0	12
GS store	12	0	12
loadm 7	0	24	24
loadm 8	0	143	143
storem 5	0	12	12
storem 7	52	110	162

Table B.9: testPrintHierarchy Macro-Benchmark Instruction Mix.

	ST	system	both
storem 8	0	143	143
ret*w's	1888	1702	3590
nonNil8-14	5682	8475	14157
int8-14	1344	4622	5966
always %skip	45	0	45
lt %skip	0	1362	1362
lt skip	7	11	18
ge %skip	0	9	9
ge skip	5	4	9
ge trap1	0	8	8
eq %skip	216	1552	1768
eq skip	51	4	55
eq %trap1	0	24	24
eq trap1	0	4	4
eq %trap4	13	0	13
ne %skip	0	5543	5543
ne skip	0	2	2
ne %trap1	0	750	750
ne trap1	0	152	152
ne %trap3	1657	98	1755
le %skip	0	108	108
le skip	377	0	377
gt %skip	0	12	12
gt skip	93	14	107
gt %trap1	0	4	4
gt trap1	0	4	4
ltu/in0 %skip	0	108	108
geu/out0 %skip	0	12	12
geu/out0 %trap1	0	370	370
geu/out0 trap1	0	1154	1154
geu/out0 %trap2	303	6	309
leu %skip	0	182	182
gtu %skip	0	108	108
out1 trap1	0	2	2
untaggedImm %ret	0	237	237
untaggedImm %retw	0	36	36
untaggedImm %retn	109	256	365
untaggedImm retn	0	8	8
untaggedImm %retnw	200	390	590
untaggedImm retnw	545	2273	2818
untaggedImm %reti	0	338	338
untaggedImm %retiw	0	143	143
untaggedImm %retinw	0	3	3
untaggedImm %skip	0	1983	1983

Table B.9: testPrintHierarchy Macro-Benchmark Instruction Mix.			
	ST	system	both
untaggedImm skip	81	0	81
untaggedImm %trap1	0	8	8
untaggedImm %load	2504	7300	9804
untaggedImm load	0	890	890
untaggedImm loadc	1657	117	1774
untaggedImm %loadm	0	167	167
untaggedImm %xor	0	370	370
untaggedImm %and	0	887	887
untaggedImm %add	728	9243	9971
untaggedImm add	441	1	442
untaggedImm %sub	13	2067	2080
untaggedImm sub	23	417	440
untaggedImm %extract	0	891	891
untaggedImm %insert	0	288	288
taggedImm %skip	35	1752	1787
taggedImm %trap1	0	370	370
taggedImm %trap2	303	6	309
taggedImm %trap4	13	0	13
taggedImm %load	404	1882	2286
taggedImm %and	0	241	241
taggedImm %or	13	195	208
taggedImm %add	37	669	706
srl barrel shifter savings	0	647	647
forwarding cost	3166	18485	21651
two-tone savings	6621	8649	15270
condJumps	363	2385	2748

B.3. Execution Profile Data

The data in this section were derived by modifying the simulator to sample its PC every 100 cycles, and using an awk [AKW] program to merge the samples with assembler's symbol table. Instrumenting the simulator instead of the SOAR program enables us to profile the program without altering its behavior. All times listed in this appendix are given as a percentage of the total time. For an explanation of the primitive numbers, see the Smalltalk-80 book by Goldberg and Robson [GoR83]. The more obscure labels can only be understood by reading our code.

Table B.10: test3plus4 Micro-Benchmark Execution Time.

57.1%	Smalltalk
17.9%	BCValuePrm2
16.1%	start
7.1%	Prim_81
1.8%	BehavNew
0%	other

Table B.11: testActivationReturn Micro-Benchmark Execution Time.

95.9%	Smalltalk
2.2%	WindowOverflowTrapH
1.8%	WindowUnderflowTrapH
0.1%	other

Table B.12: testClassOrganizer Macro-Benchmark Execution Time.

41.3%	Smalltalk
5.6%	WindowOverflowTrapH
5.2%	SIQuoPrm
4.8%	StringAtPrm
4.8%	Prim_60
4.7%	WSNextPutPrm
4.2%	WindowUnderflowTrapH
3.2%	SIMulPrm
2.5%	StringReplaceFromToWithStartingPrm
2.1%	lookupMethodInClass
2%	Prim_62
1.9%	SkipTagTrapH
1.9%	RSNextPrm
1.7%	SISISlPrm
1.6%	LoadcTagTrapH
1.6%	BehavNew
1.4%	BCValuePrm2
0.9%	SYS_word_fill
0.8%	SkipOnTrue
0.8%	SILTPrm
0.7%	SkipTagTrapS
0.7%	Prim_61
0.7%	Prim_110
0.6%	SkipTagTrapH!done
0.5%	blockCopy
0.4%	lookup
0.4%	Prim_81
0.4%	PSAtEndPrm
0.3%	blockArrowReturn
0.3%	FailPrm
0.2%	other

Table B.12: testClassOrganizer Macro-Benchmark Execution Time.

0.2%	insert!04!sel!here
0.2%	insert!03!sel!here
0.2%	allocSpace
0.2%	Prim_75
0.1%	methodBlockCopy
0.1%	cacheMissLookup
0.1%	StringAtPutPrm
0.1%	SkipOnFalse
0.1%	SVTrace
0.1%	SIModPrm
0.1%	Prim_83
0.1%	Prim_71
0.1%	Prim_111

Table B.13: testCompiler Macro-Benchmark Execution Time.

33.8%	Smalltalk
13.2%	lookupMethodInClass
5.5%	WindowOverflowTrapH
4.7%	Prim_60
4.7%	BehavNew
4%	WindowUnderflowTrapH
3%	SIQuoPrm
2.2%	SYS_word_fill
2%	WSNextPutPrm
1.7%	SIMulPrm
1.7%	RSNextPrm
1.5%	StringAtPrm
1.5%	Prim_62
1.5%	Prim_61
1.3%	lookup
1.3%	gsRegion
1.2%	Prim_89
1.1%	copyWords
1.1%	allocSpace
1.1%	SISISlPrm
1%	blockCopy
0.9%	LoadcTagTrapH
0.9%	BCValuePrm2
0.8%	StringReplaceFromToWithStartingPrm
0.8%	SkipTagTrapH
0.7%	SkipOnTrue
0.5%	gsStoreGSTrapH
0.5%	gsAnOop
0.4%	other
0.4%	gsAnObject

Table B.13: testCompiler Macro-Benchmark Execution Time.

0.4%	cacheMissLookup
0.4%	blockArrowReturn
0.3%	SkipTagTrapS
0.3%	SILTPrm
0.3%	Prim_81
0.3%	Prim_71
0.3%	Prim_70
0.3%	Prim_110
0.2%	methodBlockCopy
0.2%	insert!04!sel!here
0.2%	getWordSize
0.2%	eqNewNewBecome
0.2%	argumentCount
0.2%	SkipTagTrapH!done
0.2%	SkipOnFalse
0.2%	Prim_111
0.2%	PSAtEndPrm
0.1%	insert!03!sel!here
0.1%	gsSurvivors
0.1%	gsStoreGSTrapS
0.1%	gsRemembered
0.1%	SVTrace
0.1%	Prim_83
0.1%	Prim_75
0.1%	FailPrm

Table B.14: testDecompiler Macro-Benchmark Execution Time.

32.1%	Smalltalk
21.2%	lookupMethodInClass
7%	BehavNew
3.8%	Prim_60
3.7%	WindowOverflowTrapH
3.7%	WSNextPutPrm
3.5%	SYS_word_fill
3.1%	Prim_61
2.7%	WindowUnderflowTrapH
2.1%	SIQuoPrm
2%	lookup
1.3%	StringReplaceFromToWithStartingPrm
1.3%	StringAtPrm
1.3%	Prim_62
1.1%	allocSpace
1.1%	SISISlPrm
1.1%	BCValuePrm2
1%	blockCopy

Table B.14: testDecompiler Macro-Benchmark Execution Time.

0.9%	SIMulPrm
0.8%	LoadcTagTrapH
0.5%	cacheMissLookup
0.5%	SkipOnTrue
0.5%	Prim_71
0.5%	Prim_70
0.4%	TryRight
0.3%	other
0.3%	SkipTagTrapH
0.3%	Prim_81
0.2%	methodBlockCopy
0.2%	SVTrace
0.2%	SILTPrm
0.2%	SIEQPrm
0.2%	Prim_111
0.1%	insert!03!sel!here
0.1%	eqNewNewBecome
0.1%	SkipTagTrapS
0.1%	SkipTagTrapH!done
0.1%	SkipOnFalse
0.1%	Prim_75
0.1%	Prim_74
0.1%	Prim_73
0.1%	Prim_68
0.1%	Prim_110
0.1%	FailPrm

Table B.15: testPrintDefinition Macro-Benchmark Execution Time.

38%	Smalltalk
13.3%	WSNextPutPrm
11.1%	Prim_60
5.1%	StringAtPrm
4.9%	StringReplaceFromToWithStartingPrm
4.4%	SkipTagTrapH
3.8%	BehavNew
3.5%	Prim_62
2%	BCValuePrm2
1.8%	SkipTagTrapH!done
1.5%	lookupMethodInClass
1.5%	SkipTagTrapS
1.5%	SYS_word_fill
1.3%	SISISIPrm
1.1%	blockCopy
0.8%	Prim_81
0.7%	insert!04!sel!here

Table B.15: testPrintDefinition Macro-Benchmark Execution Time.

0.7%	allocSpace
0.5%	WindowUnderflowTrapH
0.5%	StringAtPutPrm
0.4%	lookup
0.4%	insert!03!sel!here
0.3%	SkipOnTrue
0.3%	Prim_70
0.1%	start
0.1%	StoreGSTrapH
0.1%	SkipOnFalse
0.1%	ReturnGSTrapS
0.1%	Prim_71
0%	other

Table B.16: testPrintHierarchy Macro-Benchmark Execution Time.

23.9%	Smalltalk
17.7%	WSNextPutPrm
16.6%	lookupMethodInClass
10.4%	StringReplaceFromToWithStartingPrm
6%	BehavNew
4.2%	StringAtPrm
3.1%	WindowOverflowTrapH
3%	SYS_word_fill
2%	WindowUnderflowTrapH
2%	Prim_60
1.5%	BCValuePrm2
1.3%	lookup
1.3%	blockCopy
1%	SISISIPrm
0.9%	ReturnGSTrapS
0.8%	Prim_62
0.6%	Prim_81
0.6%	Prim_61
0.4%	cacheMissLookup
0.4%	Prim_71
0.3%	start
0.3%	allocSpace
0.3%	SIMulPrm
0.2%	StoreGSTrapH
0.2%	SkipTagTrapS
0.2%	ReturnGSTrapH
0.2%	Prim_70
0.2%	Prim_110
0.2%	LoadcTagTrapH
0.1%	methodBlockCopy

Table B.16: testPrintHierarchy Macro-Benchmark Execution Time.	
0.1%	insert!04!sel!here
0.1%	StringAtPutPrm
0.1%	SVTrace
0.1%	Prim_74
0.1%	Prim_73
0.1%	Prim_111
0.1%	FailPrm
0%	other

Index

The MIT Press, with Peter Denning, general consulting editor, and Brian Randell, European consulting editor, publishes computer science books in the following series:

ACM Doctoral Dissertation Award and Distinguished Dissertation Series

Artificial Intelligence, Patrick Winston and Michael Brady, editors

Charles Babbage Institute Reprint Series for the History of Computing, Martin Campbell-Kelly, editor

Computer Systems, Herb Schwetman, editor

Explorations in Logo, E. Paul Goldenberg, editor

Foundations of Computing, Michael Garey, editor

History of Computing, I. Bernard Cohen and William Aspray, editors

Information Systems, Michael Lesk, editor

Logic Programming, Ehud Shapiro, editor; Fernando Pereira, Koichi Furukawa, and D. H. D. Warren, associate editors

The MIT Electrical Engineering and Computer Science Series

Scientific Computation, Dennis Gannon, editor

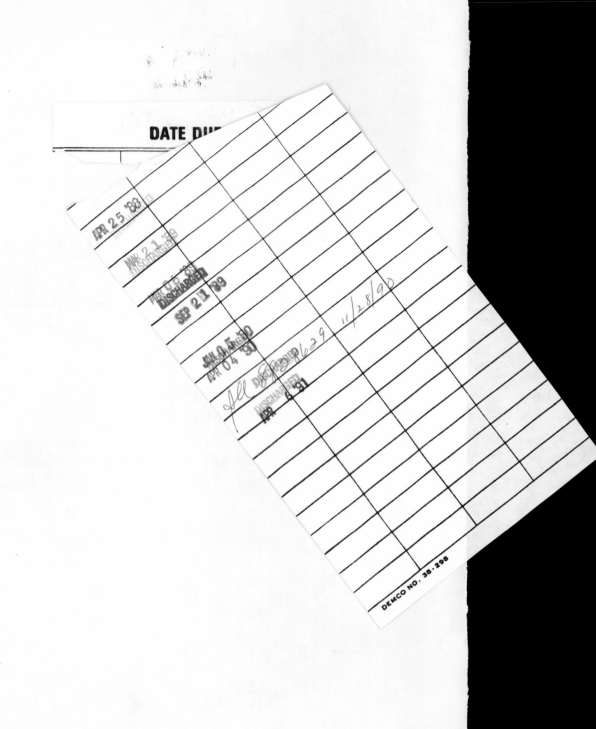